Eight Approaches to Teaching Composition

Eight Approaches to Teaching Composition

Edited by

Timothy R. Donovan
Northeastern University

Ben W. McClelland
Rhode Island College

National Council of Teachers of English
1111 Kenyon Road, Urbana, Illinois 61801

Book Design: Tom Kovacs

NCTE Stock Number 13036

It is the policy of NCTE in its journals and other publications to provide a forum for the open discussion of ideas concerning the content and the teaching of English and the language arts. Publicity accorded to any particular point of view does not imply endorsement by the Executive Committee, the Board of Directors, or the membership at large, except in announcements of policy, where such endorsement is clearly specified.

Library of Congress Cataloging in Publication Data
Main entry under title:

Eight approaches to teaching composition.

Bibliography: p.
1. English language—Composition and exercises.
I. Donovan, Timothy R., 1945- II. McClelland, Ben W., 1943-
LB1576.E34 808'.042'07 80-20474
ISBN 0-8141-1303-6

Contents

Acknowledgments

We wish to thank the National Endowment for the Humanities, William B. Coles, Jr., and the participants in his NEH Summer Seminar at the University of Pittsburgh, where the groundwork for this book was laid. We would also like to thank the Rhode Island College Faculty Research Fund and the Office of the Dean of Arts and Sciences for grants that allowed us to pursue the book further.

We are grateful to the following people for their sound advice on various parts of the manuscript: the staff of the NEH Institute on Writing at the University of Iowa, including Carl Klaus, Richard Lloyd-Jones, Cleo Martin, and Paul Diehl; Charles Cooper, University of California at San Diego; and Patricia Bizzell, College of the Holy Cross.

Finally, special appreciation is due to a number of people for their extensive help in editing and preparing the manuscript: Paul O'Dea, Director of Publications, NCTE; Philip Heim, Project Editor, NCTE; Ruth Francis Donovan; Natalie DiRissio; and Arlene Robertson.

Introduction

> Miss Groby taught me English composition thirty years ago. It wasn't what prose said that interested Miss Groby; it was the way prose said it. The shape of a sentence crucified on a blackboard (parsed, she called it) brought a light to her eye. She hunted for Topic Sentences the way little girls hunt for white violets in springtime.
>
> James Thurber
> *My World and Welcome To It*

In recalling his turn-of-the-century composition teacher, Thurber reminds us as well of the traditional writing class. The single-minded school teacher preserving literary culture and etiquette in the name of good writing. Young ladies and gentlemen heeding stylistic precepts, selecting correct words and punctuation, mimicking gracious prose. Grammar study, of course, or "drill," the foundation of rigorous language training since the Middle Ages. Many of us were taught in this way, and often taught well, we would like to think. In fact, today's perceived crisis in literacy tends to evoke nostalgia and a call for "back to basics." But the clashing—and somewhat dated—metaphors of Thurber's portrait reveal something wrong. For while our teachers were hunting down topic sentences and crucifying their shapes on the blackboard, they often failed to wonder how sentences were first shaped in their students' minds. That, presumably, was left to the muse's inspiration, or lack thereof.

Miss Groby's methods were part of a milieu that is passing, going the way, as Thurber put it, of "T-squares and rulers whose edges had lost their certainty." The problems with writing certainly have not changed, but our ways of dealing with them are beginning to. As Susanne Langer has observed, "It is the mode of handling problems, rather than what they are about, that assigns them to an age." Moreover, the mode of handling problems is characterized by the kind of *questions* that are asked, and not necessarily by the answers. Before, we might have asked, what are the forms of good writing? Today we have begun to ask, how is good writing performed? Indeed, the current question does mean less certainty for teachers. Yet it most surely directs us to consider not just the quality of writing we want from our students but also the anterior qualities of mind and behavior implied in the term *composition.* In other words, it turns our attention from the exercise of praising and blaming the writer to the more profound activity of making the writing.

This change is occurring now for many reasons, but, most of all, because enough teachers have seen that it is necessary. Just why a discipline discards a theoretical model, or paradigm, in favor of another is discussed by Thomas Kuhn in *The Structure of Scientific Revolutions* (1970). A paradigm holds sway in a profession when most of its members share the same values, recognize the same problems, and agree on similar solutions. But in time, unexplained violations of the model, or anomalies, may subvert the paradigm; questions are raised which have no meaning in the old paradigm. Practitioners must then seek new answers, which lead toward the development of another paradigm. Sometimes several paradigms compete for supremacy over a discipline until one emerges preeminent.

Until recently the field of composition has been sustained by attention to the written product and to questions about the presentation of that product. But anomalies have become apparent: the weak correlation between grammar instruction and writing ability; the conflict of social, ethnic, and regional dialects with the standard dialect; the limitations of negative criticism and editorial marginalia; the frustrations of dedicated teachers; the alienation of students. As a consequence, the traditional paradigm has been challenged to such an extent that, as Richard Young (1978) and Patricia Bizzell (1979) have asserted, we are now in the midst of a paradigm shift. Many researchers have moved their focus from analyzing surface features of composition to demythologizing the composing (or writing) process itself. Several notable studies, including those by Janet Emig (1971), Charles Cooper and Lee Odell (1978), Donald Murray (1968), and James Britton (1975), indicate that the static model, composition as formalist criticism, must evolve toward a more fluid model, composition as creative art, rhetorical versatility, and language development. They also suggest that our metaphors for teaching must be less threatening, must reflect the discovery, exploration, and settling that writing involves.

Teachers proceeding within this new model have a more realistic conception of writing, and offer their students a better chance to control the generative power of words, sentences, and paragraphs. They are not likely to begin with the notion of correctness, nor incorrectness for that matter. They know that writing doesn't come full-blown on a page, that writers must draft and re-draft, achieving (to borrow a phrase from mathematics) "successive approximations" of the ideal product. So teachers start with classroom activities which are writer-centered; they subtly guide students through the composing processes; and they skillfully intervene in those processes when appropriate. They are no less demanding of precision in form and idea, but appreciate that the structure of the writing—and any measure of correctness—must arise out of the emerging meaning and purpose of the work. In short, they teach *both* process and product.

On the other hand, this break with tradition has not by any means produced a consensus on how writing should be taught. Several "schools" of composition, many of which are represented in this volume, are thriving simultaneously, while being modified as current theory and practice dictate. Perhaps one will become dominant. But, at present, there is no best way to teach writing, especially if "best" here means empirically verifiable and universally applicable. There *is* a growing body of revealing information about sentence combining, writing behaviors, evaluation procedures, and so on. However, such statistical data must always be interpreted according to someone's definition of good writing or good teaching and it is not always applicable to every educational context. Moreover, teaching is, like writing itself, an art that depends less on formulas than on a blend of knowledge, skill, and creativity. Indeed, if anything, the new paradigm requires that teachers be flexible enough to respond to students as individuals and be ready to pursue any appropriate methodology.

Yet teachers must still develop a coherent approach that is based soundly in theory and that succeeds in practice. No approach can accomplish everything. Each is fashioned according to the specific problems it addresses and the solutions it eventually derives. In the field of composition, everyone encounters similar problems ("exemplars," Kuhn would call them) that, in effect, form the basis of our profession because they constitute our common concerns and our common language: topic and paragraph development, stylistic and syntactic maturity, rhetorical aims and modes, manuscript conventions, and others. Certainly all of these are important; however, all cannot be equally important for all students. Had we world enough and time, perhaps they could be. But much of what any teacher can do is fated by teaching style, sense of language, and simple time-constraints. The question, as Kuhn puts it, is always constant: "Which problems is it more significant to have solved?"

No two approaches can deal with all the problems, nor are they likely to deal with the same problem in the same way. Though, say, *prewriting* may be essential to the composing process, teachers may justifiably interpret it differently in terms of the role it plays in overall student writing, the writing of any individual student, or a particular classroom strategy. Consequently, one teacher may have students identifying topics, another appraising audience, a third establishing point of view—and using different strategies to do so—all in the pursuit of *prewriting.* (Similarly, in the literature class, teachers may approach *Hamlet* from a number of critical perspectives: historical, biographical, psychological, formal, linguistic, and others.) Every teacher must therefore evolve a suitable approach based upon realistic priorities and expectations.

This is, of course, easier said than done. It involves experience, research, trial and error. But one might begin, as Langer (1957) suggests, by raising appropriate questions, those, for example, that illuminate the nature of teaching and learning in general and various approaches to writing in particular. One might start out with two basic, commonsensical, and here slightly modified, questions proposed by Young (1978) in evaluating theories of invention. First, does the approach do what it claims to do? That is, does it adequately account for the writing processes of students and provide appropriate methods for improving writing ability? And secondly, does it provide a *more adequate* account and methodology than other alternatives?

Beyond these, we suggest three categories of questions to develop or evaluate an approach to the teaching of writing.

1. *Is it accessible?* That is, does it portray itself in terms that are reasonably clear and sensible? Can it be apprehended by all who must work with it: teachers, students, administrators? Are the goals, features, and limitations of the approach distinct: Does it have a high degree of generality so that it may be broadly applied? Can it be modified and still work, or is it too intricately wound? Is it thoroughgoing within its stated objectives? Is it fertile enough for further innovation, experimentation, research?

2. *Is it harmonious?* Are the objectives of the approach consistent with the means? Are all the parts consistent with each other? Are all the elements in the approach presented in the best sequence? Is the approach well-paced and balanced? Does it carefully establish expectations and the conditions for achieving a particular goal? Are the ideas and methods to be learned clearly related to the learner?
3. *Is it feasible?* Can the approach be implemented in a given classroom, at a given institution, by a given teacher? Does it meet the needs of the students, who may vary enormously—even within the same class or institution? Would it engage the students and motivate them through the term? Is it congruent with the educational philosophy of the department and institution in which it would be taught? Can it be successfully implemented given the length of time available for the instruction? Is it suitable to the general teaching style and personality of the teacher? Will addiional expertise be required to utilize the approach?

Questions beget questions, and can sometimes overwhelm. Yet they can provoke significant, even exciting options for innovative teachers and writing program administrators. The chapters that follow are intended to illustrate some of these options. To some extent they are case studies which record the authors' attempts to put it all together—at least for themselves and their students. Representing major approaches in the field, they are all similar in this respect: they exemplify some principles about the nature of composition, how it may (or may not) be taught, and, most importantly, how it may best be learned. In other words, each chapter reflects a distinct approach that carries teacher and students alike through the course.

Donald Murray begins our consideration of the composing process by describing the interactive stages of *writing* and *reading, collecting,* and *connecting.* He then sketches implications for the relationship between the teacher and the student, the student and his or her writing, the writing and the teacher. His approach is rooted in the belief that pedagogy must conform to the composing process as it truly exists, not as we might imagine or would like it to be.

The following four chapters elaborate relatively distinct approaches based upon some theory of language use or language learning that accommodates the composing process. Paul Eschholz advocates a modification of the traditional prose models approach, with its emphasis on textual form; he advises reading selections be introduced *during* the process and only if pertinent to the specific composing problems of the individual writer. Stephen Judy focuses on the writer, whose need to communicate personal feelings or experiences serves the experiential approach as a springboard for writing in the full range of discourse. Janice Lauer, working within a rhetorical approach concerned with the purposes and audiences for writing, illustrates how the teacher may lead students through a more deliberate regard for focus, readership, and revision. Kenneth Dowst takes an epistemic approach, one that considers language itself as a way of knowing, and hence writing as a way of composing one's reality. His students are motivated to see the value of writing for its own sake.

The final three chapters delineate approaches that address specific pedagogical concerns. Harvey Wiener's classroom practices introduce beginning or basic writers to process and development, not to "remedial" crash units in grammar. Thomas Carnicelli argues that the conference, rather than the classroom, is a more efficient and effective way of teaching composition and provides student comments and transcripts of conferences to help illustrate his method. Finally Robert Weiss proposes that ultimately composition must be part of a total writing environment that extends beyond the English class. He describes how a composition course may support—and be supported by—faculty and courses in other disciplines.

In a sense, these eight approaches are themselves both product and process. They are products in that the authors halt and describe what they are now accomplishing with composition and why. They are process in that they reflect the authors' continuing evolution as teachers. We should engage their ideas likewise: looking, asking, arguing, adapting; in other words, we should see products in process and process in the product.

It can happen that an author's approach fundamentally alters one's conception of teaching writing. The old ways may retain little if any charm, be judged inadequate, or even misguided. The world of writing—and the teaching of it—might then have to be remapped totally so that the road signs, the familiar terminology, point in directions consistent with the new approach. Traditional concerns (motives for writing, criteria for evaluation), terms (thesis, transition), and concepts (form, content) would have to be brought into more understandable and productive relationship. One would look in new places for answers to old problems, look in old places and see new solutions. In sum, embracing the theories, methods, and standards of the new approach, one may be inspired to an entirely different kind of teaching. Or something less dramatic—though no less dynamic—may also occur. An even more subtle amalgam of old and new might emerge.

On the other hand, one may reject a new approach, or even the ascending paradigm, wholly. Perhaps devotion to another approach, one viewed as comfortable and reasonably successful, makes the new one unattractive. Moreover, years in the classroom often create style, and style can be an effective teacher. Yet consistency, foolish or otherwise, may become mere persistence when significant trends in one's field are ignored. One risk of such rejection is professional isolation—the possibility, as it were, of persisting in believing that the sun revolves around the earth.

The approaches described in this book, then, are enactments of a sort. They evince recent thought in the teaching of composition as modified by the authors' own philosophies, research, experiences, and personalities. We should not be surprised to find differences, even disagreement. In the fabric of each, field and foreground are variously accented, movement of line is disparately cast, and colors are uniquely blended. Neither idealized success stories nor depressingly familiar by-the-numbers instruction kits, these approaches are offered in the spirit of professionals speaking to other professionals about a common commitment. They simply invite us to reconsider our own teaching, our own enactment of theory and practice in the classroom. It is through such dialogue that everyone stands to gain—but most of all our students.

Timothy R. Donovan
Northeastern University

Ben W. McClelland
Rhode Island College

Eight Approaches to Teaching Composition

1 Writing as Process: How Writing Finds Its Own Meaning

Donald M. Murray
University of New Hampshire

At the beginning of the composing process there is only blank paper. At the end of the composing process there is a piece of writing which has detached itself from the writer and found its own meaning, a meaning the writer probably did not intend.

This process of evolving meaning—a constant revolt against intent—motivates writers. They never cease to be fascinated by what appears on their page. Writing is an act of recording or communicating and much more. Writing is a significant kind of thinking in which the symbols of language assume a purpose of their own and instruct the writer during the composing process.

This process has been revered—and feared—as a kind of magic, as a process of invoking the muse, of hearing voices, of inherited talent. Many writers still think that the writing process should not be examined closely or even understood in case the magic disappear. Others of us, instructed by Janet Emig (1975), attempt to understand the relationship between the chemical and electrical interaction within the brain and the writing process. I am sympathetic to both positions, but, as a writer still trying to learn my craft at fifty-four and as a writing teacher still trying to learn how to help students learn their craft, I feel an obligation to speculate upon the writing process.

The process of making meaning with written language can not be understood by looking backward from a finished page. Process can not be inferred from product any more than a pig can be inferred from a sausage. It is possible, however, for us to follow the process forward from blank page to final draft and learn something of what happens. We can study writing as it evolves in our own minds and on our own pages and as it finds its own meaning through the hands of our writer colleagues and our writing students. We can also interview our colleagues, our students, and ourselves about what is happening when writing is happening. We can examine the testimony of writers in published interviews, such as the series of books, *Writers at Work: The Paris Review Interviews,* or in journals, letters, autobiographies, biographies, and manuscript studies. We can also consider the testimony of composers, artists, and scientists. If we attend to such available testimony, we may be able to speculate, with some authority, on how writing finds its own meaning.

But a key problem in discussing—or teaching—the writing process is that in order to analyze the process, we must give unnatural priority to one element of an explosion of elements in simultaneous action and reaction. Meaning is made through a series of almost instantaneous interactions. To study those interactions within ourselves, other writers, or our students, we must stop time (and therefore the process) and examine single elements of the writing process in unnatural isolation.

The danger is that we never recombine the elements. Some teachers present each part of the writing process to their students in a prescriptive, sequential order, creating a new kind of terrifying rhetoric which "teaches" well but "learns" poorly. It will be important for both of us—the reader and the writer—to remember throughout this chapter that we are talking about a process of interaction, not a series of logical steps. As Janet Emig has pointed out to me, we need to apply technology to our writings on process —for example, printing plastic overlays, as some textbooks do to reveal the organs of the body, as a way of showing the simultaneous interaction of the elements of writing process.

If we stand back to look at the writing process, we see the writer following the writing through the three stages of rehearsing, drafting, and revising as the piece of work—essay, story, article, poem, research paper, play, letter, scientific report, business memorandum, novel, television script—moves toward its own meaning. These stages blend and overlap, but they are also distinct. Significant things happen within them. They require certain attitudes and skills on the writer's and the writing teacher's part.

The Stages of the Writing Process

The term *rehearsing,* first used by my colleague Donald Graves (1978) after observation of children writing, is far more accurate than *prewriting* to describe the activities which precede a completed draft. During this stage of the writing process the writer in the mind and on the page prepares himself or herself for writing before knowing for sure that there will be writing. There is a special awareness, a taking in of the writer's raw material of information, before it is clear how it will be used. When it seems there will be writing, this absorption continues, but now there is time for experiments in meaning and form, for trying out voices, for beginning the process of play which is vital to making effective meaning. The writer welcomes unexpected relationships between pieces of information from voices never before heard in the writer's head.

Drafting is the most accurate term for the central stage of the writing process, since it implies the tentative nature of our written experiments in meaning. The writer drafts a piece of writing to find out what it may have to say. The "it" is important. The writing process is a process of writing finding its own meaning. While the piece of writing is being drafted, that writing physically removes itself from the writer. Thus, it can be examined as something which may eventually stand on its own before a reader. This distancing is significant, for each draft must be an exercise in independence as well as discovery.

The final state in the writing process is *revising.* The writing stands apart from the writer, and the writer interacts with it, first to find out what the writing has to say, and then to help the writing say it clearly and gracefully. The writer moves from a broad survey of the text to line-by-line editing, all the time developing, cutting, and reordering. During this part of the process the writer must try not to force the writing to what the writer hoped the text would say, but instead try to help the writing say what it intends to say.

One of the most important things I have learned, for example, as this piece of writing has detached itself from my intentions and instructed me, is that revision which does not end in publication becomes the most significant kind of rehearsal for the next draft. I had experienced this in my writing and observed it in my colleagues and my students. Yet I did not understand it until I found myself articulating it on these pages. I had never before seen how revising becomes rehearsal as the writer listens to the piece of writing. It may be worth noting that if you drop the "s" in the word rehearsing, it becomes rehearing. The writer *listens* to see what is on the page, scans, moves in closely, uncaps the pen, slashes sections out, moves others around, adds new ones. Somewhere along the line the writer finds that instead of looking back to the previous draft, trying to clarify what has been written, the writer is actually looking ahead to the next draft to see what must be added or cut or reordered. Revising has become rehearsing.

This process of discovering meaning–rehearsing, drafting, revising, rehearsing, drafting, revising, rehearsing–repeated again and again is the way the writing's meaning is found and made clear. This process may be seen in Figure 1.

I had always thought of this process in rather large terms–a period of rehearsing (perhaps minutes, but more likely hours, days, weeks, months), a period of drafting (much shorter but, in the case of a book, measured in months or years), and a period of revising (which is at least as long as rehearsing). But the significant work of Sondra Perl, Director of the Writing Development Project at Lehman College, City University of New York, has made me reconsider the time in which this process works. She writes in the *New York University Education Quarterly* (1979, p. 18):

> Composing does not occur in a straightforward, linear fashion. The process is one of accumulating discrete words or phrases down on the paper and then working from these bits to reflect upon, structure, and then further develop what one means to say.

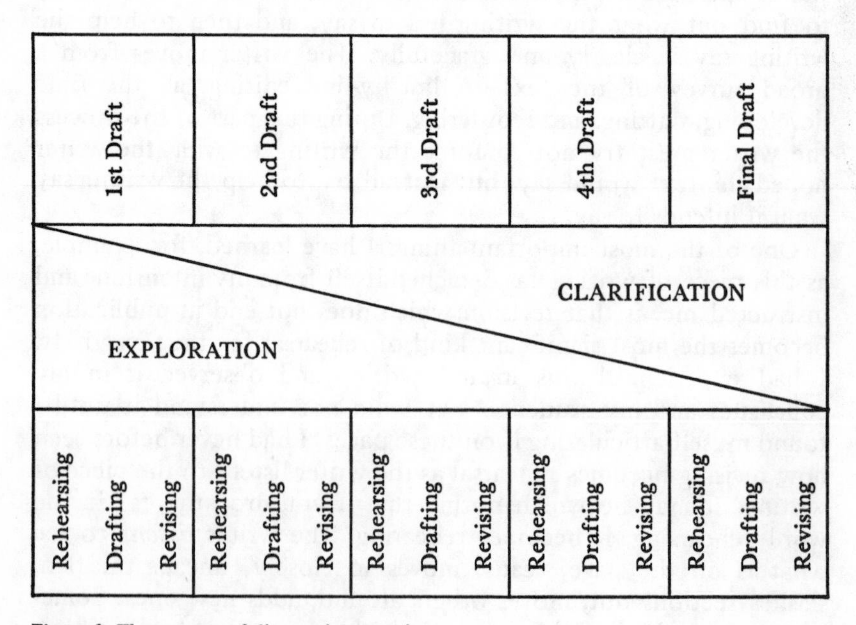

Figure 1. The process of discovering meaning.

> It can be thought of as a kind of "retrospective structuring"; movement forward occurs only after one has reached back, which in turn occurs only after one has some sense of where one wants to go. Both aspects, the reaching back and the sensing forward, have a clarifying effect. . . . Rereading or backward movements become a way of assessing whether or not the words on the page adequately capture the original sense intended. But constructing simultaneously involves discovery. Writers know more fully what they mean only after having written it. In this way the explicit written form serves as a window on the implicit sense with which one began.

Perl's work enabled me to see an instantaneous moving back and forth during the writing process. Minute by minute, perhaps second by second—or less at certain stages of the process—the writer may be rehearsing, drafting, and revising, looking back and looking forward, and acting upon what is seen and heard during the backward sensing and forward sensing.

The writer is constantly learning from the writing what it intends to say. The writer listens for evolving meaning. To learn what to do next, the writer doesn't look primarily outside the piece of writing—to rule books, rhetorical traditions, models, to previous writing experiences, to teachers or editors. To learn what to do next, the writer looks within the piece of writing. The writing itself helps the writer see the subject. Writing can be a lens: if the writer looks through it, he or she will see what will make the writing more effective.

The closer we move inside the writing process to speculate about how it works, the more we begin to see that what happens in the writer's mind seems much the same thing, whether the writer is rehearsing, drafting, or revising. We can document what happens during the rehearsing and revising process relatively well from manuscript evidence and writer testimony. We can surmise with a certain authority that what happens during the drafting process is similar; but since it happens so fast, it is often imperceptible. The writer may not even be aware it is happening.

During the processes of rehearsing, drafting, and revising, four primary forces seem to interact as the writing works its way towards its own meaning. These forces are *collecting* and *connecting, writing* and *reading.* Writing may be ignited by any one of these forces in conjunction with any other; but once writing has begun, all of these forces begin to interact with each other. It may be helpful to look at the following diagram to see how these forces interact.

These forces interact so fast that we are often unaware of their interaction or even of their distinct existence. As we collect a piece of information, we immediately try to connect it with other pieces of information; when we write a phrase, we read it to see how it fits with what has gone before and how it may lead to what comes after. To identify these forces at work within the writing process and to understand them, we must artificially halt the interaction and examine one force at a time.

The primary forward motion of the writing process seems to come from man's unlimited hunger for *collecting* information. This need grows from the animal need for food, shelter, and safety to an intellectual need to discover meaning in experience. Man is an information-collecting organism. Information, brought to us through sight, hearing, touch, taste, smell, is stored, considered, and shared. Our education extends the range of our information-collecting through reading and research that reaches back in time and across the barriers of distance and difference.

The volume of material we gather—consciously and subconsciously—becomes so immense and is so diverse it demands *connecting*. We are compelled to provide some order for the confusion of information or it will drown us. We must discriminate, select the information that is significant, build chains of information which lead to meaning, relate immediate information to previous information, project information into the future, discover from the patterns of information what new information must be sought. The connections we make force us to see information we did not see before. The connections we are making also force us to seek new, supporting information; but, of course, some of that information doesn't support—it contradicts. So we have to make new connections with new information which in turn demands new connections. These powerful, countervailing forces work for and against each other to manufacture new meanings as we live through new experiences.

The writer fears that the collecting apparatus will be excessively controlled by the connecting apparatus. Man's dread of chaos and need for order is so fundamental that writers have to resist the desire for predictable orders, and resist the instinct to fit all new information into previously constructed meanings. The writer has to encourage the gathering of contradictory and unpredictable information which will force old meanings to adapt and new ones to be constructed.

When in good working order, these forces of collecting and connecting battle each other in a productive tension that keeps us intellectually alive, working to push back the enemies, ignorance or boredom. Neither force will give the other peace. Introduce a new piece of information and the organism immediately tries to connect it. When the organism has a connection, it seeks new information to reinforce it.

There is another pair of powerful countervailing forces at work at the same time that information is being collected and connected. The force with the primary thrust is *writing.* Man has a primitive need to write. Carol Chomsky (1971) tells us that children want to write, in fact need to write, before they want to read. And indeed someone had to write during the prelude to history; that person was also the first reader. We all have a primitive need to experience experience by articulating it. When we tell others or ourselves what has happened to us, it makes that happening more real and often understandable. We need both to record and to share, both to talk to ourselves within the enormous room of the mind and to talk to others. Children—and some professors—think out loud; but for most of us, our speech is socially suppressed, done silently. Since we continue to talk to ourselves within the privacy of our skulls, some of that talking, if made public, is writing.

The act of voicing experience and connecting it involves, I think, fundamentally an aural facility. We record in written language what we say in our heads. This does not mean that writing is simply oral language written down. I believe we have a private speech we use when writing. When we know we may write, we silently practice expressing ourselves in our potential writing voices. Later we may record and revise in written language what sounded right when tried out in that silent voice within our minds. At least, this is how I think I write, dictating to myself, recording in written language what I have heard myself say milliseconds before. For many years I have dictated much of my nonfiction prose, but I was not aware until recently when I studied my own writing process that I listened to my voice while I wrote "silently" with typewriter or by pen.

Working against this powerful force of writing is the counter-force of *reading.* Put writing down on paper and it is read as it appears. Reading seems to involve criticism. We make comparisons; we look for immediate clarity, for instant grace. Just as connecting can control collecting too effectively and too early, so reading can suppress writing. The writer has to develop new forms of reading, to read loosely at first, to give the piece of writing space so that the embryonic patterns of meaning which are making shadowy appearance can have time to come clear. Writers have to learn to listen for the almost imperceptible sounds which may develop into the voice they do not expect. As the meanings come clear, the voices grow stronger. The writer has to read with increasing care, has to be critical, even surgical, but not at first.

These two forces work against each other almost simultaneously within the act of writing. In listening to the voices within our skull we "read" those voices and change them. As Perl (1979) has documented, we write and react to those marks on paper, continually testing the word against the experience, the word against the one before and the one to come next. Eventually, we extend the range of this testing to phrase, to sentence, to paragraph, to page. When I got bifocals, I had to buy lenses with an extra large reading area. They were strangely called "the executive model." But when I am writing I take them off and move my nose closer to the page. My eyes darting back and forth across my writing break out of the area bounded by my "executive" bifocals. In action writing, we do not make the separation of reading and writing that we make in school. We *writeread* or *readwrite.*

The forces of the writing process also relate to each other. This is indicated by the dotted lines in the following diagram. The act

of collecting is also an act of writing and reading. We cannot collect information and store it without naming it and reading that name. We also connect information by using language, whereby symbols carry the information. It is language which often seems to direct us towards significant connections, and we are led to them by the acts of writing and reading.

The Forces: In Balance and Out

We must always remember that each writing act is a complex instantaneous interaction. The true diagram of the writing of a sentence might look like this.

If we can manage to survive that vision after multiplying it a thousand times or more for each draft of a short essay, then we may be able to see that there is a significant sequence of balance and imbalance which takes place while the forces interact during rehearsing, drafting, and revising. During rehearsing we must give writing and collecting a slight advantage, holding off the forces of criticism and order. In revising the opposite is true. We load the dice in favor of reading and connecting. We become more critical, more orderly. The advantage holds until the balance tips. When the advantage passes again to writing and collecting, then revising becomes rehearsing.

If we see how that balance works, the scale tipped toward discovery at one time and clarification at another, then we will come to a new definition of drafting. The draft occurs when the four forces are in tentative balance. The forces have worked against each other to produce a meaning which can be read and which could perhaps be published.

In the beginning of the writing process there is no draft because the forces are wildly out of balance. The imbalance will be different with different pieces of writing, but it is there. For example, language may race ahead to the point of incoherence or be just fragmentary, a matter of notes. There may be an abundance of information which is just a jumble—no order has yet appeared from it—or there may be merely a neat, precise order, a thesis statement and outline for which there is no documentation. The process of rehearsal, however, brings the forces into balance. The writing can be read; the information begins to assume a meaningful order. The draft emerges.

The writer thinks the task is finished, that the balance will hold. But when the writer turns to read the page, it becomes apparent that the language is too stiff, too clumsy, has no flow. The reader will not follow it. Or, there is too much information; the writing goes off on tangents. Material has to be cut out and reordered. The writer may be able to help the piece of writing find its meaning through a modest amount of rewriting and researching, reordering and rereading. But many times the imbalance gets worse. The piece of writing has to follow a tangent; a new major point has to be included. Or, in fact, the major point becomes the main point. New material has to be sought out and its order discovered. The piece of writing is severely out of balance and will be brought towards balance only by rehearsing. I think it may be helpful for us to think of drafts and a series of drafts in this way, for it helps us see what has to be done to encourage a piece of writing to find its own meaning.

Continued observation and reflection upon the writing process will result in new speculations. They will come because it is our desire, reinforced by our education, to connect, to make lists, charts, maps, to find patterns and orders. This tendency is appropriate. That is what our business is. But we must remind ourselves again and again that the writing process is a kinetic activity, a matter of instantaneous motion, action and reaction which is never still. There is no clear line between the stages of rehearsing, drafting, and revising. The most meaning-producing actions may, in fact, take place on the seams between these stages when the tension between them is the greatest.

The same thing is true of the action between the forces. We do not collect and connect and then write the connection and then read it. These forces are in action against each other, and that action produces meaning. The calm, logical moment when the words stand at dress parade and present a meaning gives no hint of the battles which produce that moment—or the battles which may be ahead.

Teaching the Composing Process

In the preceding pages I have proposed a theory of how a piece of writing finds its own meaning. That theory has come out of practice. It is rooted in the experience of making meaning with written language. Theory, however, must return to practice in our field. A writing theory that can not be practiced by teachers, writers, or students and that does not produce increasingly effective drafts of writing must be reconsidered. We also have an obligation to show how the theory can be put into practice. We must show that our students are able to write more effectively and produce pieces of writing that find their own meaning because they understand what happens during the writing act. If we accept the process theory of teaching writing, then we must be able to suggest ways in which our students can experience the writing process.

In teaching the process we have to look, not at what students need to know, but what they need to experience. This separates the teaching of writing from the teaching of a course in which the content is produced by authorities—writers of literature, scientists, historians—and interpreted by textbooks and teachers. The writing teacher has no such content. It would be bizarre for the process teacher to deliver a lecture on the process theory of composition in advance of writing—just as bizarre as it would be to deliver a lecture on rhetoric, linguistics, grammar, or any other theoretical concepts before the student writes. Such information would be meaningless to the student. It might even be harmful because the student who hears such information without the perspective of his or her own experience can develop serious misconceptions about the writing process. For example, a student might get the dangerous misconception that writers know the form before they know the content, that students know what they have to say before they say it. I would not write—would not need to write—if I knew what I was going to say before I said it. I must help my students find out through a successful writing experience why that is true.

In the writing process approach, the teacher and student face the task of making meaning together. The task is ever new, for they share the blank page and an ignorance of purpose and of outcome. They start on a trip of exploration together. They find where they are going as they get there.

This requires of the writing teacher a special kind of courage. The teacher not only has to face blank papers but blank students worried by their blankness, and a blank curriculum which worries the teacher's supervisors. The teacher has to restrain himself or herself from providing a content, taking care not to inhibit the students from finding their own subjects, their own forms, and their own language.

The writing teacher who is writing and, therefore, knows how the stages in the writing process work and how the forces within that process interact, understands the students' natural desire for premature order expressed, in part, by the question, "What do you want?" The teacher must resist the impulse to respond with a prescription. It is better to explain to the students why their writing needs room—time and space—to find its own meaning.

The first day of the writing unit should begin with writing, not talking. The students write and the teacher writes. This beginning is, of course, a symbolic gesture. It demonstrates that the information in the course will come from the student. The students produce the principal text in the writing course.

It is very hard for traditionally-trained teachers who are not writing themselves to believe that students can write without instruction from the teacher or without assignment. Teachers often do not have enough faith in their students to feel that the students have anything to say. They also may not realize that much, perhaps most, of the poor writing they see in school is the product of the assignments they give. Most assignments I see guarantee bad writing. In many cases assignments direct students to write on subjects in which they have no interest and on which they have no information. They have to adopt a point of view implicit in the assignments or in the way teachers present them. They have to accept forms and perhaps languages which are not appropriate to their subjects—or their visions of the subjects.

Of course, students like assignments. Why not? They make things easy. The good students know instantly what the teacher wants; the poor students deliver as best they can. And neither group has to make a personal commitment to the writing.

It is important that the writing course which is built on the writing process set that process in action immediately. In fact, this approach might be called the writing/response method. The student writes, then the teacher and the class respond. One device I have used to begin a writing class is to hand out six 3 x 5 cards of different colors. I ask the students to take a card and brainstorm specific details about a person or place, or an event which was important to them. They may also just brainstorm random specifics. After three or four minutes I share my own list with the class. Then I ask them to circle a specific on their own cards which surprised them, or to connect two specifics with an unexpected relationship. I share my surprises with them. Then I tell them to take another card and start with that moment of surprise, or just start free writing. After three or four minutes I again share my writing with them and ask them to take another card, to continue on, start anew, or switch the point of view. And so we work through the cards. At the end we each share one card, reading it aloud without comment.

I have worked out all sorts of variations of this exercise, and so have teachers to whom I've introduced it. The important thing is that students write upon demand, that they write of what they know, that they are placed under enough pressure so they write what they did not expect to write, that the cards are small enough and switched frequently enough so they have a new chance if one doesn't go well, that the teacher shares his or her writing with them, that they listen to the voices which are coming from the members of *their* writing community and, that they discover that writing is a process of discovery.

Under such conditions I find that writing is produced. Nine hundred and ninety-nine students out of a thousand will write on demand. But if one doesn't write, not to worry. Writing is contagious. It is almost impossible to resist the desire to write in your own voice, of your own concerns, when you are part of a supportive writing community.

Sharing Writing

Once the writing is produced, it is shared. I have come to believe that this sharing, at least in the beginning, should be done orally. When students read their papers aloud they hear the voices of their classmates without the interference of mechanical problems, misspellings, and poor penmanship. Those problems will have to be dealt with in due time, but first the students—and especially the teacher—should hear the voices which come from the page.

It is equally important, perhaps more important, for the writer to hear his or her own voice. Our voices often tell us a great deal about the subject. The piece of writing speaks with its own voice of its own concerns, direction, meaning. The student writer hears that voice from the piece convey intensity, drive, energy, and more—anger, pleasure, happiness, sadness, caring, frustration, understanding, explaining. The meaning of a piece of writing comes from what it says *and* how it says it.

As the students in the writing class hear a piece of writing, they laugh with the author, grieve with the author, nod in understanding, lean forward to try to learn more. That's how the writing class begins, and that is what carries it forward. The community of writers instinctively understands that each piece of writing is trying to work its way towards a meaning. The community wants to help the writer help the piece of writing find its own meaning.

The experience of sharing writing should be reinforced by the writing conference. Individual conferences are the principal form of instruction in the writing process approach. As we have speculated upon the process by which a piece of writing finds its own meaning, we have seen how important it is to listen to the piece of writing and to pay attention to how that piece of writing is making itself heard. We must, in our conferences, help the student respect the piece of writing, pay attention to what it is trying to say, and experience the process of helping it say it.

We get the student to talk about the paper and to talk about the forces which produced the draft. We do this in conference, and we do it in workshop. I have come to believe that the workshop works best when it begins with a public conference between the writer and the teacher. The teacher gives the student the opportunity to talk about the piece of writing—what the student sees in it, what technical problems the student identifies, what questions the student has for the readers—and encourages the student to talk about the process by which the writing is being produced. The teacher initiates the conference, but soon the class joins in, writers helping writer listen to the evolving writing.

There are few lectures and large group exercises—if any—in the writing class. What is there to say until a draft is heard? Who can predict the proper response to an event which has not taken place? There are, in fact, no classes; there are workshops in which writing is shared. The writers in the workshop study drafts in process to see what meanings are evolving and, thereby, learn to anticipate what may appear on the page as well as read what has appeared.

In my own workshops I publish only the best work. The most effective teaching occurs when the students who have produced that work talk about how they have produced it. This is when I am able to show students what they have learned, and by so doing I constantly learn with them.

> How were you able to get a first draft to work so well?
>
> Well, I don't know. It just seemed to go together.
>
> Well, what did you do before you started to write?
>
> Not much. I didn't make an outline or anything.
>
> Did you think much about the piece of writing you were going to do?
>
> Oh yeah, sure. I think about it all the time, trying out different things, you know, like you're going to say at the party, or to the girl. Stuff like that, kinda' practicing in your head.

And we're into a discussion of rehearsal as I get this student, and others, to tell about how they do this in their minds and on their pages. I underline, extend, reinforce, and teach what at least some of them have already done so that they know what they've done and may be able to apply it to other writing tasks. Others in the class who have not tried it are encouraged to try it in the future.

This is the way the writing unit unwinds. The attitudes appropriate to rehearsing, drafting, and revising are expressed in conferences and in class by the students and the teacher. The skills of rehearsing, drafting, and revising are refined after they have worked successfully on an evolving draft. Concurrently, the forces of *reading* and *writing, collecting* and *connecting* are identified. The students and the teacher share their techniques for developing and controlling these forces, for helping to bring them into effective balance.

The greatest hazard for the teacher is the natural tendency not to respect the forces and instead to supply the student with the teacher's information, to make the teacher's connection, to use the teacher's language, to read what the teacher sees in the text. The teacher must remember, in workshop and in conference, to stand back and give the student room so that the student can give the writing room to find its own meaning. The teacher should not look at the text for the student, not even with the student. The teacher looks at–and listens to–the student watching the text evolve.

The teacher is not coy and does not withhold information that the student needs. But the teacher must practice the patience and restraint of the writer. The writer treats the evolving drafts with respect, trying to help the piece of writing work towards its own meaning. The teacher demonstrates this attitude by treating the student with respect so that the student will respect his or her own evolving writing. By asking helpful questions of the student, the teacher shows the student how to question his or her own drafts: "What did you learn from this piece of writing?" "Where is the piece of writing taking you?" "What do you feel works best in this piece of writing?"

Evaluation of Writing

I am always amused when people feel that a writing course is permissive, that anything goes, that there is no serious evaluation. The fact is there is much more evaluation in the writing course than in the traditional content course. Evaluation in the writing course is not a matter of an occasional test. As the student passes through the stages of the writing process and tries to bring the forces within the process into balance, there is constant evaluation of the writing in process.

This evaluation begins with each word as it is considered and reconsidered in the mind and then as it appears on the paper. The word is reevaluated as the phrase is created and recorded. The phrase is reevaluated as the sentence is created and recorded. The sentence is reevaluated as the paragraph is created and recorded. The paragraph is reevaluated as the page is created and recorded. The page is reevaluated as the entire piece of writing is created and recorded. And then the writer, having once finished the writing and put it away, picks it up and evaluates it again.

In the writing course the writer's evaluation is shared with the teacher or with other writers in the class. The evaluation is evaluated as the writing itself is evaluated. For example:

> I don't like the writing at all in this draft. It's gross.
>
> You think it's all gross?
>
> Yeah.
>
> Well, I don't think it's all gross. Some of it may be gross, but what do you think is less gross?
>
> Well, I suppose that description of how to start the snowmobile works pretty well.
>
> Yes, that piece of writing seems to know what it's doing. Why do you think it does?
>
> Well, it seems to be lined up pretty well. I mean, like it goes along, sort of natural.
>
> That's how it seems to me.
>
> Think maybe I should make the rest try to work that way? It's kind of jumbled up now.
>
> Try it if you want.

Each draft, often each part of the draft, is discussed with readers—the teacher-writer and the other student-writers. Eventually the writing is published in a workshop, and a small or large group of readers evaluate it. It is evaluated on many levels. Is there a subject? Does it say anything? Is it worth saying? Is it focused? Is it documented? Is it ordered? Are the parts developed? Is the writing clear? Does it have an appropriate voice? Do the sentences work? Do the paragraphs work? Are the verbs strong? Are the nouns specific? Is the spelling correct? Does the punctuation clarify?

There is, in fact, so much evaluation, so much self-criticism, so much rereading, that the writing teacher has to help relieve the pressure of criticism to make sure that the writer has a bearable amount. The pressure must be there, but it never should be so great that it creates paralysis or destroys self-respect. Effective writing depends on the student's respect for the potential that may appear. The student has to have faith in the evolving draft to be able to see its value. To have faith in the draft means having faith in the self.

The teacher by the very nature of the writing course puts enormous pressure on the student. There are deadlines. The student will write every day. Over my desk hangs the exhortation "nulla dies sine linea," never a day without a line, which is attributed to Pliny and which has hung over Trollope's writing desk and Updike's. I give copies of it to my students, and I practice it myself. There should, in the writing unit, be at least weekly deadlines. There is an unrelenting demand for writing.

Writing means self-exposure. No matter how objective the tone or how detached the subject, the writer is exposed by words on the page. It is natural for students and for writers to fear such exposure. That fear can be relieved best if the writer, the fellow students, and the teacher look together at the piece of writing to see what the piece of writing is saying, and if they listen to the piece of writing with appropriate detachment.

When we write, we confront ourselves, but we also confront our subject. In writing the drafts of this chapter, "How Writing Finds Its Own Meaning," I found meanings I did not expect. I suppose that I was invited to do this chapter because of the definitions and the descriptions of the writing process I have published in the past. I accepted the invitation because I had completed a new description which has since been published elsewhere. But in the months that it has taken me to help this piece of writing find its own meaning I have found new meanings. This is not the chapter I intended to write. The process described here is different from what I have described before. This piece of writing revolted against my intent and taught me what I did not know.

By the time this is published I will, I hope, have moved on. There are those who may be concerned by what they consider inconsistency or disloyalty to my own words. No matter, I have no choice. The pieces of writing I have not yet thought of writing will become different from what I expect them to be when I propose them to myself. My constant is change. My teaching changes from year to year and day to day. I do not teach my students what I have learned in the past. My students teach themselves what we are learning together.

Those of us who teach the writing process are comfortable with the constant change. This sets us apart from many people in the academic world who teach in a traditional or classical mode, believing there are truths which can be learned and passed on from teacher to student, from generation to generation. Their conception has its attractions; it is the one I was taught. But my life as a writer and as a teacher of writing leads me—as similar experience has led others—to a different tradition which some call developmental or truly humanistic. We do not teach our students rules demonstrated by static models; we teach our students to write by allowing them to experience the process of writing. That is a process of discovery, of using written language to find out what we have to say. We believe this process can be adapted by our students to whatever writing tasks face them—the memo, the poem, the textbook, the speech, the consumer complaint, the job application, the story, the essay, the personal letter, the movie script, the accident report, the novel, the scientific paper. There is no way we can tell what our students will need to write in their lives beyond the classroom, but we can give our students a successful experience in the writing process. We can let them discover how writing finds its own meaning.

2 The Prose Models Approach: Using Products in the Process

Paul A. Eschholz
The University of Vermont

Whenever we read a sentence and like it, we unconsciously store it away in our model-chamber; and it goes with a myriad of its fellows to the building, brick by brick, of the eventual edifice which we call our style. And let us guess that whenever we run across other forms—bricks—whose color, or some other defect, offends us, we unconsciously reject these, and so one never finds them in our edifice.

Mark Twain
"The Art of Authorship"

Certainly few people will take exception to the general rule that one good way to learn how to write is to follow the example of those who can write well. "You have to read, read, read," says Walter Ong (1979, p. 3). "There is no way to write unless you read, and read a lot." Professional writers have long acknowledged the value of reading; they know that what they read is important to how they eventually write. In reading, writers see the printed word; they develop an eye—and an ear—for language, the shape and order of sentences, and the texture of paragraphs. The prose models approach to the teaching of writing holds that writers can develop and improve their writing skills through directed reading. Teachers who use this approach believe that one of the best ways to learn to write is to analyze and imitate models of good writing systematically. Such study, they feel, exposes students to important new ideas and to the basic patterns of organization in nonfiction prose as well as to other specific strategies or techniques that all good writers use.

Today there are many writing programs throughout the country that use the prose models approach to help students achieve a better sense of purpose, form, and direction in their writing. Although extremely popular, the approach has received its share of criticism over the years, and much of the criticism is warranted. Critics seem not to question the value of prose models; instead, their criticism is directed at *how* and *when* teachers use prose models. I believe that prose models are important to every writer and that when appropriately integrated into the context of the writing process they become a powerful and effective teaching tool.

The Traditional Prose Models Course and Its Critics

The method of the traditional prose models approach is simple: read, analyze, and write. A typical unit in a prose models writing class might proceed as follows. In preparation for writing an essay of comparison-contrast students are asked to read Bruce Catton's "Grant and Lee: A Study in Contrasts," a classic example of this particular rhetorical mode. Next, students are asked to study the essay, answering questions about Catton's thesis, organization, paragraph development, sentence structure, diction, and so on. In class, the teacher focuses attention on the writer's purpose and his overall organization, perhaps analyzing several sample passages to illustrate Catton's "block-by-block" organizational plan or his effective use of transitions. Finally, each student is asked to write his or her own comparison-contrast essay, using Catton's essay as the model.

While greatly oversimplified, this description highlights the sequence of major activities and emphases of the traditional prose models approach. Whether looking at the entire essay or analyzing a sample paragraph or two, the emphasis is clearly on the finished product. While some teachers use the readings to initiate topical class discussions or to stimulate actual theme topics, most teachers use the readings to stress form. Their interest in form includes those aspects of writing which supposedly insure clear thinking and accurate expression: organization, thesis, paragraph structure, coherence, logic, exactness, and unity. Traditionally, the reading and discussion of an essay are necessary preliminaries to student writing. It is assumed that it is better to anticipate problems than to deal with them as they occur. In addition, students are often asked to complete brief exercises or drills that provide imitative practice and are designed to help them improve their style. These exercises follow three basic steps: students read the model sentence or paragraph, analyze the structure of the model, pointing out distinctive stylistic features, and write a sentence or paragraph in close imitation of the model. When writing their essays, students are encouraged to emulate the essays they have read and to apply what they have learned about good writing from their reading and their written exercises.

During the course of the semester or academic year, students systematically study each of the rhetorical strategies and write an essay utilizing each form. Teachers who use prose models report several advantages to this approach. Students learn the various rhetorical modes; students become better readers; students also learn what good writing is and, with varying degrees of success, apply this knowledge in their own writing. Finally, students may work through the difficult process of choosing a subject by using models as "theme-starters."

It is not surprising that the prose models approach—in one form or another—has held sway in America's high schools and colleges for the better part of this century. English teachers feel secure talking about the important themes contained in the various reading selections; discussing diction, figurative language, sentence structure, and paragraph patterns; classifying prose readings into the traditional categories of description, narration, exposition, and argumentation; and correcting student essays for syntax, spelling, punctuation, and style. Such activities go well with lecture-discussion courses which meet as a class three to five times a week; with the various textbooks (rhetoric and/or literary readers, handbooks, and sentence or paragraph workbooks) that are available; and with the skills of the majority of English teachers who have been trained to teach literature and perhaps grammar, but unfortunately not composition.

Criticism of the prose model approach does not seem to be directed at the notion of prose models *per se,* but rather at how they are used in the classroom. Several critics feel that models tend to intimidate students and that the study of models makes students feel awkward and uncomfortable about writing. They claim that the models are too good; students are overwhelmed by the distance between them and the professional writer. James Moffett (1970, p. 58), for example, feels that this situation threatens "some students by implying a kind of competition in which they are bound to lose." Students, it is argued, tend to feel at a disadvantage when forced to confront their blank paper after reading and analyzing a model.

Other critics believe that models are often inappropriate in terms of length, writing technique, and style. Why should students study a model that is many times longer than the essays that they will write and, worse yet, remote from their own writing problems? Of what use, questions Donald Murray (1968, p. 220), is a model that "only vaguely illuminates a particular kind of writing problem relevant to the student's own growth in composition"? Finally, is it reasonable or even desirable to have students imitate the styles of writers like Bacon, Milton, or Swift? While it can be argued that each of these writers has produced prose that is interesting to analyze rhetorically, their works are obviously not models of good contemporary prose and are therefore inappropriate for today's students.

Some critics question whether it is beneficial to have students read and analyze models *before* writing themselves. They question the underlying assumption that advance diagnosis of writing problems promotes learning. They feel that it is inappropriate for a teacher to intervene before the writing process has even started. These same critics object to the use of models to generate theme topics. They feel that assuming that students have nothing worthwhile to say and *must* be given something to write about before they can write grossly underestimates the capabilities of students.

Still others argue that the careful study of models places unwarranted emphasis on form and not enough on content. By studying forms and organizational patterns first students come to see form as a mold into which content is somehow poured. Students do not get a realistic view of the complex and delicate relationship between form and content in a piece of writing. They are likely to ape the models too closely and to produce mindless copies of a particular organizational plan or style. These critics argue that students have no commitment to what they are writing, and care only for how they write it. In short, these critics are suspicious of imitation and see it as stultifying and inhibiting writers rather than empowering or liberating them.

Most critics are in agreement about one very real hazard in using the prose models approach. They decry the ease with which reading becomes a substitute for writing. This substitution is especially likely to occur when literature teachers, because of enrollment demands, are required to teach writing. Without even intending it, teachers in these circumstances end up teaching reading, according to Robert M. Gorrell (1977, p. 59). Advocates of the reading-writing course, he says, assert that

> the approach provides subject matter for writing, stimulates students to write, and offers models for imitation. . . . In practice, it is perhaps more significant that teachers find the approach

> more interesting and more compatible with the literary training that most of them have had, if they have been trained in English at all. More often than not, the reading-writing course becomes a reading course with a few more or less related theme assignments, or even a course in literary history or amateur sociology. . . . If the reading dominates completely, or is not related to writing, the course ceases to be a composition course.

Finally, a growing number of critics feel that the prose models approach to the teaching of writing—with its heavy emphasis on rules, patterns, and style—has focused inordinate attention on the finished product while ignoring the composing process. The product, they assert, is only a small part of a very complex process which begins before the writer's pencil touches paper. "Teaching writers to analyze the product," according to Linda S. Flower and John R. Hayes (1977, p. 450), "often fails to intervene at a meaningful stage in the writer's performance. It fails to teach because it has nothing to say about the actual process and techniques of writing as a student (or anyone else) experiences them."

The traditional prose model approach with its emphasis on product tends to dictate rules, structures, and patterns for writers. In essence students are encouraged to know what their essays should look like before they have written them. Emphasis on the product usually leads to difficulties with the process. Because they are given no sense of priority or sequence, because they do not understand writing as a process, students are confused about how to write, and they typically try to tackle all aspects of a writing project simultaneously. They worry about the organization of ideas, spelling, paragraph development, transitions, factual information, footnote and bibliography form, and style all before writing the first sentence of what should be an exploratory rough draft.

When I began teaching writing at the University of Vermont in the mid-1960s, we used the traditional prose models approach. Our students read and talked about the essays in their anthology, faithfully worked their way through the exercises in a standard college handbook, and wrote essays modeled after a new rhetorical form every week to ten days. These essays were then collected, corrected, graded, and returned so that students could make any necessary corrections. Class time was regularly devoted to discussing themes suggested by the readings, to close analysis of the readings, and to talking about writing. Although students regularly engaged in lively discussions during class meetings, teachers began to question the success of these classes as writing classes. Why did our writing classes bear a striking resemblance to our literature classes? Were we teaching a writing course at all, or simply a course in which the students wrote (and there is a big difference)? And, was the study of prose models really working when a student could ask, "How do I write a description when I don't even know what I want to describe or why I want to describe it?" We soon realized that while the ability to recognize rhetorical strategies in reading materials might influence a student's ability to organize, it does not necessarily guarantee that the student's writing will improve.

At about the same time that we were beginning to have our doubts about prose models, we began to hear talk of writing as process from people like Donald Murray. At first glance, our traditional prose models approach with its emphasis on the study of written products seemed to be totally incompatible with—if not downright contradictory to—this new view of writing. Yet, the arguments of the process people were persuasive. Our first inclination was to abandon the prose models approach in favor of this very sensible process approach which took the mystery out of writing for students and teachers alike. But we had second thoughts. If writers—professional and amateurs alike—value reading and honestly believe that it helps them as writers, why should we be so quick to eliminate prose models from our writing courses? After carefully reviewing the criticism that had been levelled against the prose models approach, we concluded that the critics were not objecting to the models themselves, but rather to the various uses that teachers made of the readings. We felt that prose models could still serve a valuable and necessary function in a writing course. We set out to discover ways in which they could be used judiciously and purposefully within the context of the writing process approach.

Our Freshman English Committee found itself asking questions that we had never bothered to ask before. What exactly is the value of reading for the writer? When in the writing process do writers start thinking about form? What is the connection between the arrangement of ideas and the discovery of the ideas to be arranged? At what point or points in the writing process should a teacher intervene? And, how could this intervention be best accomplished? In seeking answers to these questions and others like them we found the work of Donald Murray (1968), Janet

Emig (1967), Roger Garrison (1974), William Zinsser (1980), and Donald Hall (1979) particularly helpful. And answers to these questions, in turn, helped us to redesign our freshman writing course. During the past six years, the Freshman English Committee at the University of Vermont has developed an introductory writing course in which prose models have been successfully integrated with the process approach.

Combining Process and Models

Although we still use an anthology of prose models and a college handbook in our freshman writing course at Vermont, the course is now structured by the concept of writing as process. Classes regularly meet for one or two fifty-minute sessions a week and are typically devoted to "conferencing" student papers with the entire class or in groups of three or four. Frequently, students pair themselves up for peer conferences. On a fairly regular basis students spend an entire class period writing while the instructor conducts two-minute mini-conferences with each student. These mini-conferences are particularly helpful in dealing with specific writing difficulties as the students are actually experiencing them. Rarely are class meetings used to discuss model essays; perhaps three classes a semester are used for this purpose. In addition to class meetings, students are scheduled for one fifteen-minute conference at least every other week. Students are expected to write a minimum of three to five pages per week; most write considerably more. We no longer ask students to read several essays which illustrate a particular rhetorical strategy, or to analyze the essays and then write an essay modeled after those they read.

Despite our devotion to the writing process, students are still expected to do a considerable amount of reading during the semester. While no topics are assigned and no rhetorical directives are given, students are encouraged to explore a number of topics that interest them and to experiment with various rhetorical strategies as the need arises. Prose models are introduced on an individual basis during conferences. All writing—prewriting notes, discovery drafts, revisions, and final copies—go into the students' writing folders. At the end of the semester each student submits his or her entire writing folder. Four papers which the student has selected as his or her best are evaluated. We ask only that the four papers show the writer using at least three different rhetorical strategies. In summary, the five defining characteristics of our writing course at the University of Vermont are:

1. Students learn to write by writing, and they do a considerable amount of it each semester.
2. Writing is taught primarily as a process.
3. Individual conferences are used to teach writing because they permit the instructor to address the particular needs of each student.
4. Students read widely at the same time that they are writing.
5. Prose models, instead of being presented before the writing process begins, are introduced into the process as the student needs them.

Although we spend very little class time formally discussing the reading that our students have done, reading is an important part of our freshman writing course. We expect our students to do a considerable amount of reading during the semester. They are encouraged to read widely in their anthology, and we all make an effort to suggest additional books or articles by authors who write in a style and language that students can be expected to emulate. Frequently, I am able to match a student's interests with an appropriate author—for example, Richard Selzer or Lewis Thomas for pre-med students. Annie Dillard or Rachel Carson for the environmentalists, and Roger Angell or Bill Gilbert for the sports enthusiasts.

The reading component has been retained in the writing course for several good reasons. Even though the ability to read well does not guarantee the ability to write well, through reading student-writers come to an understanding that writing is the making of reading. Too often students fail to see that what they have written is for reading; they are what Mina Shaughnessy (1977, p. 223) calls "writers producing writing." These students come to a new awareness of themselves as writers as soon as they realize that there is a writer behind everything they read. And their writing shows it, too.

Our students arrive at their standards of good writing from what they read. When provided with a steady diet of the best contemporary nonfiction, they come to appreciate what all good writing has in common. Many students are surprised to discover that the qualities which characterize good writing are the very qualities that make them as readers want to read. When their reading is informative, authoritative, clear, simple, economical, and orderly, they know that it is well-written. In good writing students hear the writer's voice, a voice that has something to say and has a reason to say it. Students also come to an understanding of the complex relationship between what someone has to say and how one says it. All of these experiences help students to dispell many misconceptions about writing. Further, they enable students to establish realistic expectations for themselves as writers.

If students are doing a good deal of writing while they are reading, it is not long before they are reading like writers. They become readers who, as Donald Murray (1968, p. 173) has pointed out, "read with a special eye for craft." Consciously or unconsciously students begin to collect their own models of good writing. As students mature as writers, they become particularly interested in how other writers solve writing problems. Students report that while they are writing they recall certain things that they have read. They are able to utilize many of the techniques, strategies, and structural designs gained from their reading.

The effects of reading on writing, however, are slow to be felt; unfortunately, there is no such thing as automatic carryover. Students must read widely and over a long period of time. But the rewards are satisfying. As Donald Hall (1979, p. 14) points out, "gradually we acquire the manners that make the good writing we admire. It is like learning a foreign language by living with a family that speaks it, by shopping in it, and by listening to television shows with dialogue in it."

Although we now teach writing as a process, we no longer feel that it is in conflict with our use of prose models. As Murray (1968) argues, if we are going to teach writing honestly, it is only fair that we look at what writers do and pattern our instruction after them. An understanding of the composing process tells us primarily that students learn to write by writing and rewriting and that students must discover what they have to say before they can determine how to say it. The process approach to composition helps to demystify writing for students. They find it comforting to know that there is a process, a series of steps, through which most writers find it necessary to pass most of the time. When the writer is trying to solve a specific problem in the composing process, however, prose models can be valuable if introduced appropriately.

The individual conference is particularly effective in this regard because it permits the teacher to intervene in each student's writing process at times when the student can use the help most. It is during these conferences that I make great use of prose models. I introduce, discuss, or suggest prose models that an individual student might find helpful in dealing with his or her particular writing problem. To supplement the readings in the anthology my students use, I maintain a collection of popular college readers as well as a file of clippings from such publications as the *New York Times, Sports Illustrated, Newsweek, Time, Country Journal,* and *The New Yorker.* Whenever I come across a piece of good writing —a striking lead, a particularly persuasive argument, a noteworthy use of specific details, a convincing example, an interesting use of analogy, or an especially effective short dramatic sentence—I file the particular passage or essay away for use with students during conferences. I encourage the students to bring to class examples of effective writing that they have found in their reading. I then add these examples to my file for use with other students.

Also, I maintain a modest library of contemporary nonfiction in my office for use by my students. It certainly is not comprehensive, but it does include a sampling of current titles, as well as some old favorites. The most popular titles of late have included the following:

Roger Angell, *Five Seasons* (Simon & Schuster, 1977); *The Summer Game* (Popular Library, 1973)

Michael J. Arlen, *The View from Highway 1* (Farrar, Strauss & Giroux, 1977)

Issac Asimov, *Earth: Our Crowded Spaceship* (John Day, 1974; Fawcett, 1978)

Rachel Carson, *The Sea Around Us* (New American Library, 1954); *The Edge of the Sea* (Houghton Mifflin, 1955, 1979); *Silent Spring* (Houghton Mifflin, 1962)

Robert Coles, *Children of Crisis: A Study of Courage and Fear* (Little, Brown, 1967); *Migrants, Mountaineers, Sharecroppers* (Little, Brown, 1972); *The South Goes North* (Little, Brown, 1972); *Eskimos, Chicanos, Indians* (Little, Brown, 1978); *Privileged Ones* (Little, Brown, 1978)

Joan Didion, *Slouching Towards Bethlehem* (Farrar, Strauss & Giroux, 1968); *The White Album* (Simon & Schuster, 1979)

Annie Dillard, *Pilgrim at Tinker Creek* (Harper's Magazine Press, 1974; Bantam, 1975)

Loren Eiseley, *The Night Country* (Scribner's, 1971); *All the Strange Hours* (Scribner's, 1975); *The Star Thrower* (Times Books, 1978; Harcourt Brace Jovanovich, 1979)

Nora Ephron, *Wallflower at the Orgy* (Ace, 1973); *Crazy Salad: Some Things about Women* (Bantam, 1976)

Peter Farb, *Word Play: What Happens When People Talk* (Knopf, 1973; Bantam, 1975)

James F. Fixx, *The Complete Book of Running* (Random House, 1979)

Bernard Gladstone, *The New York Times Complete Manual of Home Repair* (Times Books, 1978)

Edward Hoagland, *African Calliope* (Random House, 1979); *The Edward Hoagland Reader* (Random House, 1979)

Roger Kahn, *The Boys of Summer* (New American Library, 1973); *A Season in the Sun* (Harper & Row, 1977; Berkley, 1978)

Elisabeth Kubler-Ross, *On Death and Dying* (Macmillan, 1974)

Peter Matthiessen, *Wildlife in America* (Penguin Books, 1978); *Blue Meridian* (New American Library, 1973); *The Snow Leopard* (Viking Press, 1975; Bantam, 1979)

John McPhee, *The Pine Barrens* (Farrar, Strauss & Giroux, 1968, 1978; Ballantine, 1976); *The Deltoid Pumpkin Seed* (Farrar, Strauss & Giroux, 1973; Ballantine, 1976); *The John McPhee Reader* (Farrar, Strauss & Giroux, 1976); *Coming into the Country* (Farrar, Strauss & Giroux, 1977; Bantam, 1979)

Harold J. Morowitz, *The Wine of Life and Other Essays* (St. Martin's Press, 1974)

George Orwell, *Shooting an Elephant and Other Essays* (Harcourt Brace Jovanovich)

Berton Roueche, *Eleven Blue Men and Other Narratives of Medical Detection* (Little, Brown, 1954)

Carl Sagan, *Broca's Brain* (Random House, 1979)

Richard Selzer, *Mortal Lessons: Notes on the Art of Surgery* (Simon & Schuster, 1978); *Confessions of a Knife* (Simon & Schuster, 1979)

Thomas Szasz, *The Second Sin* (Doubleday, 1973); *Heresies* (Doubleday, 1976); *The Myth of Psychotherapy* (Doubleday, 1978)

Gay Talese, *The Kingdom and the Power* (Doubleday, 1978)

Studs Terkel, *Working* (Pantheon, 1974)

Lewis Thomas, *The Lives of a Cell: Notes of a Biology Watcher* (Viking Press, 1974; Bantam, 1975); *The Medusa and the Snail: More Notes of a Biology Watcher* (Viking Press, 1979)

Alvin Toffler, *Future Shock* (Random House, 1970; Bantam, 1971)

E. B. White, *The Points of My Compass* (Harper & Row, 1979); *One Man's Meat* (Harper & Row, 1944, 1978); *The Second Tree from the Corner* (Harper & Row, 1954, 1978); *An E. B. White Reader* (Harper & Row, 1966); *Essays of E. B. White* (Harper & Row, 1977, 1979)

Tom Wolfe, *The Pump House Gang* (Farrar, Strauss & Giroux, 1968; Bantam); *Radical Chic and Mau-Mauing the Flak Catchers* (Farrar, Strauss & Giroux, 1970; Bantam, 1971); *Mauve Gloves & Madmen, Clutter & Vine* (Farrar, Strauss & Giroux, 1976)

William Zinsser, *On Writing Well* (Harper & Row, 1976, 1980)

Students appreciate having these books available to them. I find that the collection generates a genuine excitement about nonfiction among students which, in turn, is reflected in their attitude toward their own writing.

Intervening with Prose Models

During the early stages of the writing process students' questions focus on the large issues of subject selection, gathering information, purpose, and organization. Prose models can be used to help students solve problems in any of these areas. As students move through second and third drafts, their questions or concerns become more specific. In conference, students readily acknowledge dissatisfaction with their beginning or ending, or realize that their tone is inappropriate, or see that the various parts of their essays are disconnected, or hear awkward repetitions when reading an essay aloud. Prose models can be used effectively in the context of the writing process to solve many of these specific writing problems.

During the prewriting stage I use prose models very sparingly. It is at this stage that student writers need to be on their own in order to discover what it is they want to say and why they want to say it. But this is not to say that prose models should not be used at all during prewriting. Some students find it helpful to see what other writers have done with similar subject matter. If asked, I try to find an article or book in the area that they have chosen. Students report that the models helped them to see the many possibilities in their subject and to focus on a particular topic within the subject area.

Once students have chosen a subject, focused on a specific topic, and gathered enough information to write a rough draft, they search for a pattern of meaning in the information. Often the writer's purpose for writing, frequently presented in the form of a question, suggests a natural structure or organization. An informal or "scratch" outline helps the students to visualize a form—a chronological sequence, a spatial order, or some logical arrangement. Because of their previous training, many students early in the semester feel that they need a thorough outline in order to write a rough draft. It is not long before they realize that the very informal scratch outline gives them enough sense of form to serve their purposes at this point in the writing process. It is best, I feel, to leave form tentative during the prewriting stage because it will evolve naturally as students discover exactly what it is they want to say.

There are, however, students who find a definite sense of structure absolutely necessary in the prewriting stage because structure restricts "the area of thought," as Lucile Vaughan Payne (1966, p. 30) argues, "thus bringing mind and imagination into full play in relation to a single idea. Paradoxically, it frees by restricting." For these particular students—and their numbers are not great—it is helpful during the prewriting conference to discuss their purpose for writing and to point out appropriate essays or parts of essays that illustrate patterns they could emulate. Last semester, for example, Mary, a student who wanted to describe her two grandmothers who had lived in her family's house while she was growing up, found it helpful to read several model descriptions in Mary McCarthy's *Memories of a Catholic Girlhood* before writing her descriptions. The models helped her to see that in order to create a dominant impression descriptive details had to be carefully selected and arranged. It was tempting to me to suggest to Mary that perhaps what she had in mind was a comparison/contrast of her two grandmothers. But I knew that it was important for her as a writer to describe each grandmother fully first, for in describing the grandmothers she might discover what it was she wanted to say about them.

While actually writing their rough drafts students will encounter problems that can usually be resolved in a brief conference. Students can be sent to an appropriate prose model when a question of form occurs. Once they have decided what they want to say and why they want to say it, they must decide how most effectively to say it. Although questions of form are most common, other interesting questions come up. Jim, a student who happened to be writing a personal narrative about a ski accident, came to my office somewhat disturbed one day this semester. His paper was a first person narrative, and he was extremely uncomfortable about using the first person pronoun in his piece. One of his high school teachers had told him never to use "I." Together we took a look at Langston Hughes' "Salvation" and the opening paragraphs from George Orwell's "Shooting an Elephant." The models made their point very effectively, and Jim left my office reassured.

Harry came to my office for a conference on his second paper. He had been thinking about writing one on John, the owner of the local barbership, and had almost completed a rough draft. While he liked his topic (it seems that John was somewhat of a neighborhood curiosity), he was disappointed in the draft. Harry told me that his rough draft was flat and didn't go anywhere. He felt that he was forcing the description, that he was telling not showing. After reading several short "profiles"—the kind that frequently appear in local newspapers and weekly magazines—Harry realized that he should talk with John before attempting to write his rough draft. The factual information and human interest quotations that John gave Harry were just what he needed to put life into his essay.

Once my students have produced rough drafts, I feel that it is appropriate for me to intervene with a conference discussion of form as it relates to content. As Richard Larson (1976, p. 71) soundly advises

> instead of talking about "good organization" in the abstract, or advocating one plan of organization in preference to all others, the teacher should recognize the interconnections of form and content, and help students quietly in the subtle and personal task of choosing a form that suits well their ideas and emphases. Since reliable criteria for such choosing are not available, flexibility and sensitivity to the values of different structures are attitudes to cultivate. Form may not *be* the message, but it interprets the message while relaying it. And we all need, basing our best judgment on sensitive reading of our drafts or finished essays, to consider *how* our message is relayed and interpreted through its form.

During a conference on their rough draft, students frequently discover that what they now want to say about their subject is not what they had originally intended to say. Their purpose has changed and the new purpose demands a new structure. Such was the case with Mary, the aforementioned student writing about her two grandmothers. In considering her rough draft she discovered that she was not as much interested in describing each grandmother as she was in relating the similarities of these two very different women. Before starting a second draft, she would benefit from reading several of the comparison/contrast selections in the anthology. She knew that she had all the information she needed; it was simply a matter of reorganizing it to fit her new purpose.

Prose models are particularly effective in dealing with problems of voice. In the early weeks of every semester, several students, especially those students who lack confidence in themselves as writers or those with some skill who want to play it "safe" for awhile, will write "voiceless" papers, the type that other students respond to by asking, "Where are you in this essay?" This semester Marian came to a conference with a voiceless paper about her decision to attend the University of Vermont over four other colleges and universities. After talking with her briefly about the paper, I asked her to read it aloud. Next I asked her to read aloud the passage from Annie Dillard's *Pilgrim at Tinker Creek* in which a frog is eaten by a giant water bug. Marian immediately recognized what she had to do in her revision and did it.

I spend a significant portion of class time having students read and discuss the various drafts of their own essays. Without any prompting on my part students often make useful references to their outside reading or to model student essays while discussing each other's papers. They recall in great detail how an author solved a particular problem and point out the appropriate passage for the student whose paper is being discussed. For example, this year Frank had trouble describing his favorite possession—his motorcycle. Because he was so familiar with it, he found it impossible to get the distance he needed. It was obvious to the students in the class that Frank's description lacked specific details. But how could he say something specific about something that was so familiar? One student read aloud the opening paragraph from *Five Seasons* in which Roger Angell describes a baseball in great detail. The model helped Frank solve his problem.

The number of ways that prose models can be used in the revision process is endless. If a student continues to have difficulty using specific information, I have found it useful to have the student read a paragraph or two that rely heavily on specific details, underlining each piece of specific information encountered. I then ask the student to compile a list of specific information that could be used in writing his or her own essay. I have experienced some success in using paragraph-length models to help students work on their openings, use figurative language to enhance a description, show and not tell, give full examples to support a generalization, and develop unified paragraphs. As students get closer to a final draft, their attention begins to focus on the little things that make a difference. Difficulties with transitions, diction, dramatic short sentences, parallel structure, and strong action verbs, for example, can be easily handled with short prose models.

At all stages in the writing process, prose models have worked for me and for my students. The main problem with the traditional prose models approach has been that teachers tend to present the models too early in the writing process. Too often students are asked to read and study models before they have written a word; a form is assigned before they know what they want to say. It has been assumed that problems are best solved before they ever arise. But writing does not work that way. Students must be permitted to discover their own writing problems. Models can be a positive and useful device in teaching students to write better if they are thoughtfully and purposefully integrated into the individual student's writing process. Writers can best learn from what other writers have done when they find themselves in similar situations. Teachers (as well as students) need to read with a writer's eye and to develop a file of models that can be used in their own writing as well as in their teaching. With practice, any teacher will gain confidence and skill at using problem-specific prose models in the writing course.

3 The Experiential Approach: Inner Worlds to Outer Worlds

Stephen Judy
Michigan State University

> The development of the personality is inextricably bound up with the development of language.
>
> Andrew Wilkinson
> *Spoken English*

> That is why I started to write. To save myself. . . . I had to seek out the truth and unravel the snarled web of my motivations. I had to find out who I am and what I want to be, . . .
>
> Eldridge Cleaver
> *Soul on Ice*

> The neat thing about writing . . . is that paper allows us to get our feelings in control, help ourselves understand exactly what we mean.
>
> Ingrid Crachiola, student
> Central Michigan University

The experiential approach takes as its intellectual center the complex relationship between language and thinking, and further, the relationship between experience and language and thinking. That language, thinking, and experience are, to use Wilkinson's phrase,"inextricably bound up" with one another has long been recognized, but it is only within this century that the relationship has begun to be fully explored. For earlier rhetoricians and psychologists, the connection seemed much simpler. In the nineteenth century, for example, language was widely held to be a "mirror" of thought or the "clothing" in which one "dressed" ideas. If the writing teacher accepted this conceptualization, his or her functions were comparatively simple. Errors in language represented errors in thinking and were to be eradicated. Stylistic infelicities represented a failure to choose the proper garb for one's ideas and were to be corrected quickly, just as one would correct inappropriate table manners. Nineteenth-century teachers thus gave unusual attention to mastering the forms of language—rhetoric or grammar—and relatively less to actual practice. In no small measure, these attitudes toward language, experience, and thinking formed the basis of present practices emphasizing formal correctness at the expense of ideas and content.

In the twentieth century, psychologists—most notably Piaget, Vygotsky, Langer, Jung—and teacher/linguists—Chomsky, Britton, Korzybski, McLuhan, among others—have differently described a more complex relationship between mind and language, between thinking and speaking or writing. While language obviously "reflects" thought, there is no one-to-one correspondence between word and thought. Perceptions are shaped and influenced by past experiences and by the language one has learned. Thinking, which was once held to be a neatly logical process, is recognized as a symbolic process, and as such, it involves inaccuracies that are introduced whenever one represents (or symbolizes) one thing by another. Thinking, experiencing, and languaging are thus a kind of eternal triangle—but a flexible triangle, a rubber triangle—bound together, yet influencing one another.

For most people, this rubber triangle is constantly growing and stretching. Every day the person—adult or child—has new experiences: seeing, tasting, hearing, reading, watching TV, and so on. Those experiences are internalized and in a language-based process synthesized to become part of the person's storehouse of experience. When one faces a new problem or concern, he or she draws on that storehouse and through the complicated activity labeled "thinking" (also a language-based process) comes up with "ideas" or "solutions." Finally, the person creates language about his or her ideas that both displays them for self-examination and allows them to be communicated to others. What gives this process its drive—its energy—is, first, that humans have an intrinsic need to sort through and understand their experiences, and second, that they need to share their perceptions with others.

Major Premises

From the discoveries of linguistics, psychology, and rhetoric about the relationship of experience, thinking, and languaging, there follow certain major premises informing the experience-based approach to teaching composition. I present these premises informally at the beginning of all my writing courses so that the premises do not remain my secret.

The best student writing is motivated by personal feelings and experience. That one should "write from experience" is, of course, a scholastic truism, advice given by just about every composition teacher at one time or another. But in practice the maxim is often distorted. On the one hand, the students' experiences are often trivialized, as in the infamous "My Summer Vacation" theme that forces writers to present superficial or irrelevant experiences. On the other hand, teachers assume that because students are young, they have no significant experiences and ideas and must therefore be "primed" before writing. In one form, this lack of respect for the students' experience leads to "stimulus writing," where young people are "charged up" through the use of clever or gimmicky activities, then set loose to write. At its worst, it leads to the conventional research paper assignment where students struggle to master a large body of information that is duly (and often dull-ly) recorded on paper.

Students of all ages have a wide range of experiences that can serve as the starting point for writing: hopes and fears, wishes and ambitions, past events in their lives, even fantasies. What seems most important is that students recognize that whatever they write—be it personal confession or a description of how to program a computer—should grow from fully synthesized experience. Writing from experience does not preclude either "serious" writing (e.g., exposition) or writing about new knowledge (research). To write well, one must know something well. Bad writing, whether in personal or abstract language, results when one has not worked with (and played with) his or her ideas and experiences.

An obvious implication for the teacher of composition is that students need to draw on and develop their base of experience. The teacher must provide time for students to talk about, to expand, and even to relearn or reexamine their experiences. While students occasionally need to write impromptu themes, especially on examinations, their writing will be considerably better if the teacher provides ample time for thinking and planning prior to writing.

Writing from experience takes place in many modes of discourse, including creative forms, but by no means excluding expository and academic modes. I want my students at any level—elementary, secondary, college—to compose in as many different forms as possible. I would like them to write poems, plays, stories, essays, and, if they are up to it, novels. I also want them to compose in nonprint forms, through film, video, or sound tape. As McLuhan has argued, "the medium is the message." It is clear that the same or similar messages come out differently in different media. A poem says things differently than a song does. An essay opens up possibilities not available to the writer of an objective report. Language forms, conventions, and rhetorical styles place some limits on what a writer can say, but they also open up possibilities for saying more or less the same thing in different ways.

I am convinced that writing in many different modes is, in the long run, practical for students, even though in "life" the student may be limited to writing the academic exam or the business memo. When school and college writing programs give the students a sense of the full range—the play—of discourse, those students are better equipped to deal with even routine writing tasks.

Writing from experience often, but not invariably, requires that students write for a readership. The readership will often be someone other than the instructor. Some writing is private, done, as Cleaver says, "to seek out the truth and unravel the snarled web of my motivations." Writing allows one to set down ideas and contemplate them in peace and quiet before going public (or deciding to remain silent). The success of the writing journal in both school and college writing courses attests to the need of young people for this kind of private writing. Nor does the need diminish with age. Therapists and counsellors of adults have recognized the value of journal writing, and many use it as part of their program.

At the same time, people naturally seek out an audience for their writing. Students' initial shyness about making writing public should not be confused with a desire to keep things private. Even journal writers have a craving to let others read and respond to their work. In many classes, the students voluntarily break the shroud of privacy that their teachers have offered for journal writing. What begin as private journals become common class reading before long.

The teacher should be *a* reader of student writing, but not the *only* reader. Students' comments to one another can be at least as helpful as the teacher's, while at the same time being less threatening. When students write for "real" readers—their classmates or people outside class—they pay more than usual attention to matters of form, style, and correctness. Writing for an audience allows students to see such matters as an aid to reaching readers rather than simply as a teacher's concern or obsession.

The structuring of writing is learned as one shapes ideas and experience, first, for himself or herself, and second, for an audience. "Form" in writing has traditionally been presented as something independent of a writer's content, indeed, as something which exists before content. For instance, generations of students have been taught an idealized form of the paragraph, then told to match their writing to that model. For over a century, young people have been shown the formal outline and told to make their compositions fit in. In contrast, I tell my students that form grows from content and is inseparable from it. One doesn't simply pick a form and match ideas to it. Rather, the writer looks at experience, meditates about it, thinks over the aim and purpose of the piece, considers the background and interests of the audience, and gradually begins to evolve strategies for shaping—for *form*-ing—his or her work. True, there are conventions of form and style in writing—from the "paragraph" to the "stanza"—and the writer must be conscious of those traditions and the resultant reader expectations. But the *fiat* holds: Create a form that will work for your content and this audience at this time; don't look about for a ready-made structure.

Many good writers report that the discovery of an organizational pattern is a mystery. Ideas gather and percolate; the writer thinks over some beginnings and endings; he or she may start and discard some drafts. But eventually, the "eureka" moment happens. A workable plan occurs or presents itself and the writer is off and running. That process of organizing can't be taught, but it can be fostered, catalyzed, and practiced through an experience-based approach. Certainly teachers should avoid setting up false or inaccurate structural models.

As students explore the full range of discourse forms and compose for a variety of audiences, form and correctness can be explored. These days many observers charge that composition teachers tend to ignore correctness in favor of something called "self-expression." Teachers who consider themselves part of the "experience-based" approach often find themselves under attack in this light. In one faculty meeting after another, I have heard something like this: "There are some teachers in this school [or university] who tell students that misspellings and improper usage are perfectly OK; the only thing that matters is what you think."

But try as I will, I have yet to discover a teacher who admits to holding that precise philosophy. I doubt that such mongers of unbridled creativity exist. I know of no teacher who claims that correctness absolutely "doesn't matter." Most teachers try to place correctness in reasonable proportion to content and expression.

The debate over correctness is much too complex to discuss here, since it involves socio-political concerns as well as linguistic matters. But it is important to recognize that an experience-based approach does not ignore correctness. Rather, it treats correctness in the context of actual composing experience for genuine audiences. Students take correctness into account when writing for audiences other than the teacher. Their concern for mechanics and usage is part of the problem of preparing *this* paper "here and now" for *this* audience at *this* time. Errors are best dealt with on a "need to know" basis, with the teacher supplying editorial advice and suggestions as required to help the student find success in reaching his or her readership.

Learning to write "correctly"—and more generally, learning to become conscious and deliberate about form and style—is a gradual process. I believe that the schools are in much too big a rush to try to solve every young person's problems of form instantly. From the time they enter school, children have every error, every flaw, every blight pointed out to them. The net effect has been to create generations of students who "can't" write, which means simply that they cannot relax sufficiently *to* write. A good experience-based writing program, one which diversifies writing modes and audiences, will create enough good, solid writing experiences that in the course of twelve or more years of schooling, students will master the forms of correctness they need to know to function effectively in their unique worlds.

The Writing Workshop

There are many ways the premises of an experience-based approach could be worked out in classroom practice. To exemplify one way, I want to describe an experience-based college course which I taught recently. It was a sophomore-level course at Michigan State University called simply, "Writing Workshop." The catalog description reads: "A writing workshop designed to help students improve their writing abilities. The course provides opportunities for students to write with different purposes in a variety of modes."

Given such a broad description, the students enrolled with diverse expectations. Some took the class simply because an intermediate writing course was required for their major or minor: "Take a writing course. Any writing course." Others enjoyed writing and were interested in extending their abilities; the promise of a writing "workshop" appealed to them. Many—the majority—enrolled because they were not succeeding as writers within the university, and they wanted help beyond what their freshman course had given them. The students presented a range of ability levels. Dan was a bright political science major who could write fluent gobbledygook and had received too much praise for slick, but empty, prose from earlier teachers. Bob was an agriculture major taking the course to meet a requirement, not because he saw any earthy [sic] use for it. Helen, an adequate writer, had centered her life on her membership in the marching band and would write only about her music. Diane was a bright, advanced-placement freshman who had opted out of freshman writing. Though she was a good writer, she was caught up in being away from home and suddenly in love with a junior from Detroit and could write about nothing but that. None of the students in the course was an English major.

I began by explaining my premises for teaching writing. I knew from past experience that at one point I would have to do a sales job: convincing the students that writing in a variety of modes and on personal topics would help them with their university courses. "I promise you," I said, "that before the term ends we will spend time discussing the particular problems you face as a psychology major or music major or physics major. We'll talk about how to write better examinations and term papers. But before you can be a good writer in your major, you have to become a good writer, period."

Most of the students tentatively accepted that argument. Some didn't and the best I could do was ask them to reserve judgment. In the end, I believe most were persuaded.

My second selling job was a far more difficult one: persuading the students that they had something to write about. Like most writing students from grade six on up, these students believed—or, more accurately, had become convinced—that they had nothing to say. Given a set assignment—"Analyze the major causes of the Civil War"—they could struggle through on the basis of textbook knowledge, but given an invitation to write—"Write about something that is important to you"—they felt they would founder.

To overcome this problem, I gave them an interest inventory. It presents a number of topical categories and asks the students to free associate, writing down what comes into their heads. The topics include *friends, enemies, people you admire, special places, fond memories, not-so-fond memories, worries, strange-but-true stories, sports, university life, books, television, music, film,* and *what matters most.* None of the students had any real problems coming up with five, ten, or more items under each category. "Those," I explained, "are your starting points for writing. Everything on that list—*memories, films, friends, enemies*—is the beginning of a story or essay that another person will be interested in hearing or reading."

They were dubious, of course, but we plunged in, and for the next several weeks they mined those lists for writing ideas. We discussed "Where do first drafts come from?" I described some of my own idiosyncracies and struggles over drafting papers, and compared quotations from "name" authors who described their writing agonies. We reviewed some basic "getting started" strategies that seem to work for many students: Peter Elbow's "freewriting"; stream-of-consciousness writing based on a key word or phrase; talking aloud to oneself; borrowing a lead sentence (in which the writer uses another person's opening sentence, but substitutes his or her own content). Many of the students' writings were short, sometimes just a paragraph in length. About half the writings were done in class, about half outside. The length of the pieces gradually increased as the students grew more and more confident of their ability to use their own experience as the stuff of writing.

Because of the terrible self-consciousness college students (and, I'm afraid, most novice writers and many pros) have about their work, I did not, at first, ask the students to read one another's papers. I read everything. Sometimes I read outside class, in which case I wrote notes back to the student; often I read in class, simply collecting essays and reading them back to the class without revealing the author's name. That oral reading sometimes involved oral editing as well, and I would make a few minor revisions as I read if, on the spur of the moment, I thought they would clarify a paper. The point of these "instant replays" was to show the students that even at the rough draft stage their writing could be lively and interesting. I made a point of emphasizing what struck me as especially well chosen words or ideas.

Eventually the students read one another's work. There was only one ground rule: readers were to respond to but not critique the paper. They were to describe their own reactions to the events and emotions presented on paper, not to offer formal evaluation. Initially the students read and responded in pairs. As the term progressed, the discussion groups grew to four or five students. Eventually, papers were presented to and discussed by the entire class.

The culminating activity for this first phase of the course was the writing of a major paper drawing on personal experience. (There were no firm limits for length or number of words. The students generally wrote between five and ten pages.) I encouraged them to write something along the lines of a sustained reminiscence or memoir because new writers seem to appreciate the distance between themselves and their experience that writing in the past tense allows. To prime the pump, I brought in excerpts from three books describing childhood memories: Harper Lee's *To Kill a Mockingbird,* Lincoln Steffens' *The Autobiography of Lincoln Steffens,* and Mark Twain's *Life on the Mississippi.* We talked a bit about the techniques of these writers, but we principally tried to soak up the tone of these rich, detailed, loving remembrances. The students talked over their preliminary ideas with one another and with me.

After time for the writing of initial and second drafts, the students submitted their papers, which were, I thought, quite good. A piece on marching with the band was written at this time, as were reminiscences of family life, school, church, the first term of university life, even early childhood. One student, borrowing from Evgeny Yevtuschenko, submitted a chapter of his "precocious autobiography." At least some of the students were willing to read their pieces to the whole class. In *Uptaught* (1970), Ken Macrorie describes telling his students that each of them will, during the term, write something that will truly knock his or her classmates for a loop. Some of my students had that experience that day.

For the second phase of the course, I borrowed an idea expressed by J. W. Patrick Creber in *Sense and Sensitivity* (1965, p. 23) that "much . . . inarticulateness has its roots . . . in a blunted sensibility." Young people, he claims, fail to perceive and synthesize their experiences fully. (I suspect he could agree that many adults have the same problem.) As a result, he says, they write thinly, in cliches. In the language of the experience-based approach, this means that people do not so much lack experience as they lack the ability to see and appreciate its fine details.

This second phase of the course was titled "Interweaving the World," drawing on a phrase James Miller, Jr. and I used in *Writing in Reality* (1978). I sent the students outside the classroom to study and write about their environment. They engaged in "people watching" and wrote character sketches; they spent hours in places around town—libraries, the student union, taverns—observing the environment and learning to turn their perceptions into words. The course took on a journalistic flavor. The students were, like newspaper writers, to find stories in their daily lives.

At this point, the range of discourse forms from which the students could choose was widened. (To date, they had written only narratives and personal essays.) "But," I explained, "there are many different ways in which you can put experience into words. Sometimes an observation will work better as a poem than as a story. A personal experience can be depersonalized and turned into a piece of fiction. A simple observation of characters and setting can lead you to develop a play."

I urged the students to try some new forms, to try some creative writing. To ease their anxiety, the writing in this phase was called "experimental." Some of the students were immediately ready to take a risk and wrote in genres that were, for them, completely new—fiction, fantasy, poetry. (I did not dwell at any length on the formal characteristics of these genres; rather, I relied on the students' intuitive sense of rhetoric developed through their reading.) Other students were less willing to gamble and continued to write first-person narratives and descriptions. However, with one or two exceptions, all the students genuinely explored the ranges of discourse, moving away from the familiar to test out new ways of putting their ideas into language. Most of those who tried were successful, especially when they were able to get editorial help from their classmates.

At this time I encouraged the students to respond as informal critics to one another's work. Since the papers were "experimental," it was appropriate for the writers to seek help from one another. I argued from deep conviction that their responses could become as helpful to the writer as anything I or another teacher might say. The students were initially to concern themselves only with content, rather than with grammatical or mechanical correctness. Their motto was a piece of advice from a graduate student at Michigan State: "When you edit, don't try to be superhuman. Don't try to fix everything. Just apply your strengths to the places where the paper needs the kind of help you can give."

A great deal has been written about the advantages and drawbacks of peer- and small-group editing in recent years. There *are* problems. Some students use it as an opportunity for an ego trip at the expense of their colleagues. Others don't have the writing skills to help their peers. Some are too inhibited either to present a critique or to receive criticism. Others have been indoctrinated into believing that only the teacher's advice counts. Nevertheless, peer-editing does help students move outside their own writing to view it with a degree of detachment. Most important, it helps writers learn to function independently so that when they write outside the confines of a composition course, they have the skills and the confidence to serve as their own editors.

As a culminating activity for this second phase of the course, the class put together a magazine. Each student selected what he or she took to be the best piece of writing done for the course to date and, working with a small group, edited it for publication. A day was devoted to discussing correctness, the need for it in published work, and the distinction between *revising* a work, which is changing content and language, and *copy editing,* which is correcting problems in syntax, style, mechanics, and usage.

The university budget being what it is, the publication itself was not elaborate. The pages were mimeographed, dittoed, and photocopied—each student was responsible for bringing in multiple copies of his or her work. An art major in the class cut a linoleum block and printed a number of covers on heavy paper. A short poem by one of the students was chosen for the cover, and this was overprinted beside the linoleum block using the mimeograph. The whole booklet was held together with brads. Publication day was, in a sense, a non-teaching day, because both students and teacher simply sat and read, all enjoying their accomplishments in their own ways.

The third phase of the course was given over to helping the students work on academic writing problems. Good writing in college (or in the "real world") is not created by a fundamentally different process than the narrative and perceptual writing in which the class had been engaged. Too often college writing courses present academic writing as formula writing, especially in the scientific and technical fields. This group of students responded to the notion that good academic writing, like a good poem or short story, grows from a fully synthesized experience, a deeply known and even *felt* experience.

The students studied, each in his or her own discipline, the basic kinds of writing that are required and the way that writing is generated. Many of the students interviewed professors in their major area. Virtually all collected papers they had previously written, and some interviewed other students in their subject-area classes. In each instance, they raised the question: "How do ideas in the discipline find their way into language?"

The students reported back to the class. A chemistry major showed how a professor's experience in the laboratory—something having to do with amino acid interface chemistry—was refined and developed into a theory, tested through further experimentation, presented as a speech at a major convention, and eventually published as a paper in the *Journal of the American Chemical Society.* A history major told how a historian blends primary and secondary sources to form a historical construction, first in his or her mind, then on paper for a historical journal. A music major treated music itself as a language and demonstrated how one of her ideas for a musical composition had been translated, first into black notes—"words"—on a page, then into actual music: "language." In the process of conducting this research, the students observed many of the conventions of writing in their disciplines, and more important, came to understand why those conventions had come into being. This, in turn, had practical implications for their day-to-day college writing.

Next the students worked on a subject paper of their own. It could be a paper that had been assigned for another course, or it could be an original paper on a topic which interested them. By having studied the processes of exploring, researching, and writing in the disciplines, they were better able to understand and conform to the constraints that are unique to the subject.

The students refined their editing skills further by again working in small groups. For this assignment, the students could play the role of the "dumb" editor, that is, one who knows next to nothing about the topic. While playing dumb, the respondents helped writers see precisely where and why their messages were or were not coming through.

Most of the students worked on papers that had been assigned for other courses. In several instances, students were worried that they would be guilty of plagiarism or of not having "done the work myself." So they checked out our project with their professors, who, in every instance, were delighted that their students were able to get help outside of class.

In the final phase of the course, I circled back to where I had begun: to the self as the center of the writing process. Again borrowing a phrase from *Writing in Reality,* I spoke with the students about "Writing and the Ultimate Self" and related their efforts to the Brihararanyaka Upanishad, which says, "By knowing the self . . . through hearing, reflection, and meditation, one comes to know all things." This served to remind the students that experience is at the basis of all writing. It is "the ultimate self" that one puts down on paper. As Donald Murray (1968) has said, writing is an *ethical* act. It comes from discovering who one is and portraying a vision of the self, as clearly and honestly as possible. I also quoted William Faulkner's Nobel Prize acceptance speech: "The poet's voice need not merely be the record of man, it can be one of the props, the pillars to help him endure and prevail."

For the final writing assignment, the students did something that would have been a disaster at the beginning of the course: write a paper on anything they chose. The only ground rule was that the paper had to reflect their vision of their "ultimate" selves, which is to say, the paper had to be on something they felt strongly moved to say. They took off in many directions. One student finished up several chapters of his precocious autobiography, exploring his relationship to his parents in depth. The band student did a careful piece describing how one gets two-hundred-and-fifty people maneuvered into the shape of a Mississippi River steamboat or a likeness of Darth Vadar in fifteen seconds or less while everyone plays "Here Comes the Showboat" or the theme from *Star Wars.* The art major wrote a number of poems and illustrated them. A science major picked up on some work he had done for a science fair in high school and did additional reading research about it.

The students might have run off multiple copies of these papers for a second class magazine, but the papers were too diverse to fit legitimately between covers. Instead we turned to bookbinding. Using a method that is common lore for many teachers, I showed my students how to cut, stitch, and glue cardboard and cloth to make an attractive hardbound cover for their final writing.

"I want you to remember this piece of writing and save it," I said in presenting the project.

I believe they will.

Individual Growth and Language Growth

Many readers will recognize that my course followed the inner-worlds-to-outer-worlds pattern that one finds described in the works of Piaget, Creber, Moffett and others. In their discussions it is applied to children as they grow from childhood to adulthood. At first, children are egocentric, with a limited ability to project themselves beyond their own concerns. Eventually they move toward other-centeredness which allows them, as young adults, to objectify and abstract from their worlds and to relate to the feelings of others. As they grow psychologically, their language matures as well, so that sophistication in language follows and emerges from sophistication in perceiving and dealing with experience.

This pattern can usefully be repeated as the structuring principle of a writing course. The embryologists say that "ontogeny recapitulates phylogeny," that the history of the individual repeats the evolution of the species. The inner worlds/outer worlds pattern, valid as it is for human growth in a broad sense, works nicely for individual writing courses as well.

The same basic pattern, with appropriate modification, can be used with younger students. In my secondary school textbook series, *The Creative Word,* (1973, 1974) each book (or "course") begins with the private exploration of personal experience and moves toward public writing dealing with a broad range of topics. What makes each course different is the psychological and linguistic maturity of the students. The intent is to offer the student at any level an opportunity to explore and experiment with both the richness of his or her mind—the ultimate self—and the full dimensions and resources of composition.

The course I have outlined is, in many respects, eclectic, drawing on and incorporating concepts from many schools of thought in the teaching of writing. It treats writing as *process* in such a way that the "experience-based" approach is consistent with the "writing process" approach advocated by Donald Murray. Also, the course assumed a *learn-by-doing* philosophy: that writing is learned through actual practice, not principally through rule study or error correction. *Peer editing* and *self assessment* were key concepts. Students learned to evaluate and analyze their own writing, rather than depend on others to do it for them. The course aimed at *integrated* language study by incorporating literature and by treating the students' own writing as a form of literature. I introduced *interdisciplinary* concerns, so that composition touched on many subject areas and was not limited to something called "English." Finally, *rhetoric,* considerations of invention, form and arrangement, style, and audience, were a natural part of the course.

An eclectic approach need not—*must* not—lead to an *a*theoretical hodge-podge. The electicism of the experience-based approach finds its unity in the student/writer. In the long run, what matters for them is not the absolute quality of what they write, but whether or not the writing experience contributes to their growth as human beings. If growth in the individual takes place, growth in language will naturally follow.

4 The Rhetorical Approach: Stages of Writing and Strategies for Writers

Janice M. Lauer
University of Detroit
Marygrove College

Rhetorical theory and research on writing, an evolving body of knowledge, shows that writing is not the mysterious process it has sometimes been taken to be but rather an art that can be taught and learned. Aristotle speaks of such an art at the beginning of his *Rhetoric*.

> Most people do so [make use of Rhetoric], of course, either quite at random, or else merely with a knack acquired from practice. Success in either way being possible, the random impulse and the acquired facility alike evidence the feasibility of reducing the process to a method; for when the practiced and the spontaneous speaker gain their end, it is possible to investigate the cause of their success; and such an inquiry, we shall all admit, performs the function of an art.

Today the art of rhetoric extends beyond oral persuasion to encompass written discourse, including such aims as the persuasive, expressive, and referential. Rhetorical theorists, incorporating the work of other disciplines which analyze the communication process, have been investigating the nature of the writing process from its planning stages through to the forms of different types of written products. With their help, our understanding of the writing process increases. Our methods of teaching writing must change to reflect this growing knowledge.

Some Pedagogical Premises

The approach described in this chapter represents *one* of many possible applications of rhetorical theory and research. It is based on the following tenets:

1. Writing is a unique way of learning and discovery whose first beneficiary is the writer.
2. The writing process extends from a writer's sense of exigency through discovery of insight, to development and revision of discourse, and on to interpretation by the audience.
3. Writing encompasses identifiable stages which are neither mechanical nor totally linear, but often recursive and overlapping. Some stages are conscious and hence admit of deliberate improvement; others are not conscious.
4. Writers adjust their work in these stages to compose discourses with different aims—expressive, persuasive, referential, and literary.
5. The art of writing involves maintaining a balance among the writer, the audience, and the subject in each unique rhetororical situation.
6. Rhetorical powers are different from conventional skills (grammar, spelling, and punctuation)—the former are capacities for choice guided by rhetorical principles and context; the latter enable adherence to the rules of a given language.

While these tenets do not dictate any specific teaching method, they do suggest important general directions for pedagogy. For example, if writing is a unique way of learning and discovery, then writing assignments should be set broadly enough to allow students to find genuine starting points and to explore questions that *they* deem compelling, whether the writing deals with personal experience, public issues, or literature. The pacing of such writing experiences should allow students time for both conscious and preconscious activity throughout the complex stages of the process. Also, teachers of writing should provide guidance *during the process* if students are to acquire the art of writing.

Offering such guidance in no way reduces writing to a mechanical performance because an art always employs advice, principle, or strategy in a way unique to each new situation. Students who work intelligently in the conscious stages of composing follow no magic formula which guarantees them new insights and successful papers. Each writing occasion calls for a different interplay of their individual background and talents with a unique rhetorical situation—audience, subject, setting, media, aim. Teaching writing as rhetorical art neither offers a recipe for good writing, nor, at the other extreme, abandons the writer to struggle alone.

Another implication of the tenets is that writers adjust their work in the stages of composing to create discourses with different aims. Composition should be taught so that students gain facility with different kinds of writing. Most important, they should learn how the powers they are developing (articulating a starting point, exploring, focusing, analyzing audience, and drafting) operate to create these various kinds of writing. In contrast with a product approach to writing, which inevitably must focus on the differences between types of discourse, the rhetorical approach concentrates on the *similarities* in the process of composing many kinds of papers.

The sixth tenet addresses the problem of teaching students with mixed backgrounds. Because rhetorical powers are different from conventional skills, students who come to college with control over grammar, spelling, and punctuation may still need to be helped to acquire rhetorical power. Unfortunately many of these students have been led to identify the art of writing with correctness, a misconception perpetuated by objective tests which exempt them from writing courses because they control the conventions. On the other hand, students who lack conventional skills should not be relegated to courses in grammar as substitutes or as prerequisites for instruction in the art of writing. Rather, remediation belongs in the context of courses devoted to developing rhetorical power. When students labor to communicate valuable insights in genuine writing situations, they see the importance of control over conventions and benefit more from remediation.

Theoretical tenets such as those discussed above offer broad directions for teaching; they do not provide specific *strategies* to guide students in their work. Such strategies are necessary to move theory into practice, but they are not to be confused with the stages of the composing process. Stages constitute the process itself; strategies are procedures to guide students through these stages. Instructors using this pedagogy must commit themselves to helping students with the conscious stages of composing specified here, but the strategies outlined in what follows are completely open to modification. Some instructors might find them useful; others might refine them or devise their own. Students, in turn, should be encouraged to use them in highly individual ways. The presentation of stages and strategies is exemplified by one freshman's effort to write an expressive paper.

Finding and Articulating a Starting Point

Writing, like all creating, begins with an exigency, a sense of dissonance, an awareness of ambiguity, the urgency to know something unknown (Young, 1979; Festinger, 1965; Rothenberg, 1979). It starts with questions, not answers. Students who are used to being rewarded for right answers need help to awaken their questioning minds. Assigning a paper triggers dissonance—but often an artificial one, a disequilibrium which paralyzes instead of mobilizing. Writing instructors should try to pose writing contexts in which students can find *personal* exigencies. When students identify experiences, issues, or ideas that puzzle them, that exceed or fall short of their expectations or that clash with their values, their writing process starts as a personal quest for insight. To set a direction for the search, however, they need to push beyond a sense of discomfort to some understanding of their "felt" dissonance. They must verbalize it. The instructor can coach them to use a two-part strategy: (1) state the elements in the subject which clash with their values or exceed their expectations; (2) formulate a question to direct their search for a resolution.

Mary, the student whose writing process will be used as illustration, was assigned "the private world of relationships" as a writing context. She began by identifying a relationship which had troubled her for some time—a lost friendship with a girl named Debbie. She moved beyond this feeling to state some aspects of her friendship which conflicted with her values. Then she posed a question to determine what she needed to know to resolve her unease.

My values	*My relationship*
lasting friendship	Debbie was my best friend but the friendship didn't last
the self-assurance and lack of concern for the future that Debbie had	she shot herself

Question: Why, after being so close, did our lives go in different directions? Why did Debbie commit suicide if she was so self-assured?

She shared her starting points with the instructor and the class in an effort to determine whether the question captured her dissonance and offered direction for inquiry.

Exploring Using Heuristics

To stimulate memory and intuition in the search for answers, good writers use heuristic thinking, guided guessing which prompts them to recall what they already know and to discover new associations. Taking multiple perspectives, they examine their subjects broadly to expand their views and to prepare for insights. This approach suggests a strategy (adapted from Young, Becker, and Pike, 1970), which directs students to explore their subjects from three perspectives: (1) as *static:* with unchanging, distinctive features; (2) as *dynamic:* in process, changing; and (3) as *relative:* placed in classifications with other things, compared and contrasted, and associated through analogies. Mary was encouraged to use this strategy to explore her relationship with Debbie, recording her ideas in concrete and specific language. Her exploration developed the following material.

Static View

she was a friend—a "best friend" for awhile—I envied her—she seemed to self-assured, she never seemed to worry but took things as they came while I was always worried

Debbie had the following features:

blue eyes the color of blue Fostoria crystal that sparkled—long thick blond hair that hung in waves on her back (sometimes the roots were light brown)—developing breasts—she wore size B and C cups when we were all still flat or nearly so—her clothes, color-coordinated shirts, blouses and sweaters (you could tell by fabric, the lines of the clothes, the workmanship they weren't expensive)

she lived "south of 6 mile" a phrase analogous to "wrong side of the tracks" among the old families; houses there were small, frame or brick, two bedroom with none of the luxuries available in the University District (no four or five bedrooms, library, formal dining room and breakfast room)—we had the luxury of space—privacy

our relationship:

we went to school together; Debbie was bored by it, sneaking down the alley or over to White Tower for a cigarette

spending the night; sitting up late, smoking cigarettes, exchanging confidences (we never talked about the future though—it was about Leo and had he called, who was he going with now, we carried a torch for him for four or five years, both of us or Steve, or Matt "the Phantom" so skinny he would slip in and out of places unnoticed til he was there or gone)

Dynamic View

became friends in sixth grade—went to the same school—in high school we went to different schools but spent a lot of time together—we drifted apart toward end of high school—trading in old friendships for new ones creeping down the stairs and out-of-doors to meet some guys and party in the middle of the night, we seldom got caught

she'd invite me home from school for lunch—her mother sitting in the dark (shades drawn) in the living room, beer in one hand, cigarette in the other watching the afternoon movie or a soap opera—two places neatly set in the kitchen with place mats, plates, soup bowls, silver, napkins, sandwiches already made for us and hot soup waiting in a saucepan on the stove

Debbie dancing—to some rock group—her body shifting, gliding, every part moving effortlessly, relentlessly to the driving beat of the bass guitar

Debbie—with laughing eyes, welcoming her older brothers home on leave from the navy

Debbie—hiding under the bed in an upstairs room from the police, called into a party which got too rowdy, a beer brawl, while I stood quaking in the hall and lied to the policeman (who thought I was too young and frightened to have been a participant) "I didn't see anyone come up but I was back there"; my knees scarcely held me up; he flashed his light in the closet carefully looking behind the clothes, and into every corner of the room, before leaving

I saw her once when I was eighteen in Sandy's Coney Island (stayed open til 4 a.m., a hangout for drug culture children, with its black ceilings, poster-covered walls, juke-box playing acid rock so loud you could hardly hear over it)

Debbie's hair was tangled, mousy brown, worry lines around her dull blue eyes, perspiration-covered face "Do you have any money? Mickey's going to cop (means buy). I need $20.00." "Only 35¢" (a junky-heroin addict)

I never saw her again

from a friend a year later I heard she shot herself in the head

Relative View

1. Contrast

Debbie:

she was working-class—greaser (teased hair, heavy make-up, cheaper clothes)—school bored her, criticized my vocabulary as having too many big words—lived for the day, the moment, acted on instinct, emotion

Me:

I was middle-class—flat, short conservative hair, not much make-up, expensive tailored clothes—secretly enjoyed classes, reading books—believed in solid middle-class, delayed gratification, never could rid myself of the nagging thoughts about possible consequences—although I tried for years

2. Classification

a 1930s detective novel would call her a "tough cookie"—a sensitive friend, she never laughed—a loyal friend

3. Analogy
like a coconut, rough, prickly exterior, tough to crack, warm sweet milk on the inside

When the students have explored as fully as they can, the instructor reviews their work, pointing to avenues of further inquiry, encouraging a more specific and concrete record of ideas.

Discovering and Stating a Focus

With a compelling starting point and a thorough exploration, students have a chance for an insight, a new understanding of the subject under scrutiny. Because insights spring from the preconscious, students need time for incubation, time between exploring and drafting. They also need help with converting an insight into a focus in order to determine if it eliminates the dissonance, answers the question, fits in with past insights. To do this testing, the instructor may suggest that each student use the strategy of formulating the insight into a two-part focus: (1) the subject or part of the subject that appears important and (2) the point of significance, the new understanding. If this articulation satisfies the writer, he or she has a working focus for a paper. Mary formulated her insight into the following focus:

Subject	*Point of Significance*
My loss of friendship with Debbie and her eventual suicide	were due to her ability to live according to the impulses of the moment and her inability to see future consequences

The student should submit at least one focus to the instructor who can help determine if the formulation clearly expresses the significance the student has been seeking and now wants to communicate.

Planning for Aim and Audience

Meaningful insights give students something worth sharing with an audience. Some situations dictate the audience. Others allow a choice. In any case, writers must take stock of their audiences, looking for bridges of communication and ways of reducing threat. To help with the analysis of the audience, students can be given an audience guide. Such a guide would direct them to:

1. study the audience in itself:
   a. its political and social background, education, expertise
   b. its value system

2. determine the audience's knowledge of the subject and attitude toward it
3. decide the role the audience will play in relation to their voice as writers: peer to peer, authority to subordinate, other

Mary chose her audience, analyzing it with the guide:

1. Audience: I want to write this for myself because I've asked myself why her and not me over and over again
   a. middle-class, teen-ager, high school education, part of the drug culture
   b. values—people over property, intellectual growth, friendship
2. no opinion as to cause until I'd finished the exploration, just vague impressions and memories
3. I'm writing as a peer to a peer, a participant trying to sort through all the memories in a more objective way

Once again, the instructor should review the students' work, pointing out aspects of the audience that need further analysis, noting potential bridges for communication.

Writers also need help in determining their aim (Kinneavy, 1971), that is, the concern of the discourse with the audience (persuasive aim), the writer (expressive aim), the subject matter (referential aim), or the form itself (literary aim). Often this aim is set by the writing situation or assignment. Research and critical writing, for example, usually require a referential aim. Mary's paper had an expressive aim which guided its development and her stylistic choices.

Organizing and Developing the Paper

To assist with the difficult task of organizing, teaching writing as a rhetorical art shows students that the patterns of four modes of discourse (Kinneavy, Cope, and Campbell, 1976)—description, narration, classification, and evaluation—can be used to structure papers having any of the aims. Because these patterns admit of endless variation, they equip students with more flexible ways of organizing than the straightjacket of the five-paragraph theme.

The writer's work in earlier heuristic stages provides resources and direction for development. The exploration already contains much that will support a focus. The aim, focus, and audience will guide the selection of material. In this case Mary relied heavily on her exploration for supportive details and examples. As she drafted her paper, she worked on choices of diction and syntax appropriate for an expressive aim. Because she had struggled during exploration to record her ideas in specific and concrete language, she had a stock of diction from which to draw for her first version (see next page), which she organized using the narrative mode.

Critiquing and Rewriting

Having created first versions with as much craft as they can muster, students need time and advice to tackle revision. Criticism from peers and role playing of intended audience by the instructor can provide valuable guidance for revision. To direct such critiquing, a Critical Guide may direct students to comment on the writer's (1) adherence to focus, (2) development of the aim for the audience, (3) organization and coherence, (4) choices of syntax and diction, and (5) maintenance of conventions—grammar, spelling, and punctuation.

Revision differs under this approach from the extensive drafting of "free writing." Here the "freer writing" of the earlier stages has already led to a working focus. Revision is not, therefore, drafting for insight. Nothing prevents students, however, from recasting a focus at this stage, if rewriting so prompts them.

A small group responded to Mary's first version, indicating that they felt her development was sufficient to give the audience an insider's view of the relationship and its changes. They advised her to relate her first two paragraphs more directly to her focus and to repair the break in the narrative organization made by the introduction of the classification of "tough cookie." They liked her concrete diction but felt she should check for redundancies. Finally, they argued over the first paragraph, some feeling it was an intrusion of an artificial introduction into a narrative mode, others liking the initial summary.

On the basis of these and other comments, Mary revised her paper, including among the changes the elimination of the first paragraph and the repair of the narrative by inserting the classification into the narrative framework:

> At these parties Debbie didn't seem to worry about the future. She might have been described in the 1930s as a "tough cookie" because she lived according to the impulses of the moment. If we got . . .

A Lost Friend

Debbie was a friend during that part of adolescence when a girlfriend means more to girls than parents, teachers, or even boyfriends. We took those terrifying, exhilarating first steps toward growing up together but Debbie never finished the journey. She shot herself in the head and died before she turned twenty-one.

I can't remember when we first met but we became friends during sixth grade. Debbie was beautiful then with sparkling eyes the color of blue Fostoria crystal and long thick blond hair that hung in waves down her back (sometimes the roots were light brown). She wore color-coordinated skirts and sweaters which you could tell by the fabric, the lines and workmanship were not expensive. Underneath her sweaters you could see her developing breasts--B and C cups when I was still flat. I looked ordinary, nondescript, with mousy brown hair and glasses. Sometimes Debbie would set my hair, tease it up, comb it out, help me apply heavy black eyeliner, blue eye-shadow and mascara and then I felt older, sophisticated like her.

Although we went to the same school together I can't recall ever talking about it with Debbie. School bored her and she sometimes criticized my vocabulary for big words. She often invited me for lunch though, and we walked from school to her house "south of 6 mile" a phrase analogous to the "wrong side of the tracks" among the local aristocracy. The houses there were not as large as ours and the people not as wealthy. When we arrived, Debbie's mother would be sitting in the shade-drawn living room, a cigarette in one hand, a beer in the other, watching the afternoon movie or a soap opera on television. In the kitchen two places would be neatly set with place mats, silver, plates, soup bowls, and glasses. We helped ourselves to the sandwiches waiting on the counter, the hot soup simmering in a saucepan on the stove and a glass of milk. After lunch we sneaked down the alley or over to the White Tower for a cigarette before returning to school. I took quick shallow drags on my cigarette and stubbed it out hastily, certain that someone would see us smoking.

When high school began Debbie and I went to different schools but we saw even more of each other. After school we usually met at some friend's house to listen to 45 rpm records. I can still see Debbie dancing to some rock group, her body shifting, gliding, every part moving effortlessly, relentlessly to the driving beat of the bass guitar. She tried to teach me but I was awkward, ill-at-ease and a slow learner.

On weekend evenings Debbie often spent the night at my house. We sat up late, smoking cigarettes, exchanging confidences. We never talked about the future though; it was about Steve or Matt "the Phantom" who was so skinny he could appear and be gone unnoticed or most often about Leo. We each had dated Leo for several years and we'd talk about who he was going with now or if he called or if we had seen him somewhere. When my parents were sound asleep we would creep down the stairs, out the door through the quiet night-time streets to whatever party was going on that night.

Debbie might have been described in the 1930s detective novel as a "tough cookie." She lived according to the impulses of the moment. She didn't seem to worry about the future. If we got a ride to a party in the suburbs Debbie enjoyed herself while I worried about how we'd get home. If we were out in the middle of the night Debbie had a good time while I was sure my parents would find out or we'd get picked up by the police for breaking curfew. Usually my fears were needless but once the police were called into a party which got too rowdy, a "beer brawl." Debbie hid under the bed in an upstairs room while I stood quaking in the hall and lied to the policeman (who thought I looked too young and frightened to have been a participant). "No one came up here." He flashed his light in the closet, carefully looking behind the clothes and in every corner of the room before leaving. Debbie crawled out from under the bed laughing at my quavering voice and colorless face. For her the danger was over while I spent days fretting over what might have happened.

I can't remember when we stopped being "best friends"; it happened gradually. When I was eighteen I saw Debbie in Sandy's Coney Island, a hangout for drug culture "freaks" with black ceilings, poster-covered walls, and a juke-box that played acid-rock so loud that you could hardly hear over the music. Debbie's hair was tangled, mousy brown, and there were worry lines around her dull eyes. Her face was covered with perspiration and I could tell she needed a fix.

"Do you have any money? Mickey's going to cop and I need $20.00."

"Only 35¢. You can have that if you want."

She left soon after and I never saw her again. A year later someone told me she was dead. Sometimes when I think of her now I wonder if she never worried because it didn't occur to her that anything could go wrong or if she didn't care if it did.

After revision, students may submit this second version for evaluation, together with their work in the previous stages. To respect the complexity of the process, the instructor should provide students with assessments of their work in the planning stages as well as in each category of the Critical Guide, such as focus, development, organization, style, and conventions. Giving students multiple evaluations on a revision differs significantly from branding their first effort with a single grade. Instead of reducing their work to a compromise, factor evaluation praises their successes and identifies their weaknesses. Grading then becomes an important instructional tool.

Implementation

Structuring a course based on this approach requires neither elaborate materials nor esoteric methods, but instead relies on such basic teaching techniques as:

1. introducing students to each stage and strategy, using student examples
2. holding practice sessions in class so students can try the strategies on sample subjects
3. engaging the students outside of class in the actual process leading to their own finished papers
4. responding to students' work at each stage as they progress

These methods determine the pacing of the course, the nature of the classroom activity, and especially the content of assignments. Each class session concentrates on preparing students for their current phase of writing. The pacing allows students sufficient time for careful work in each stage, for incubation, and for teacher responses. All assignments engage students in phases of an evolving paper.

Teaching writing as rhetorical art changes the roles of teacher and student. The instructor acts as a guide and enabler, responding to students' work at each stage, commending, advising, and encouraging *during the process,* rather than merely criticizing the finished product. Students are no longer mystified by unstated expectations but become more confident and deliberate inquirers and symbolizers once initiated into the art of effective writing.

5 The Epistemic Approach: Writing, Knowing, and Learning

Kenneth Dowst
University of Iowa

A few years ago, a young woman in my general composition class, a freshman, composed this essay on "College Life So Far":

> I've never really been away from home before, so there certainly was a great deal of apprehension about coming out here. Very little of the past two months here have helped me to adjust comfortably.
>
> Somehow, thanks to my messed up advisor, I am the proud possessor of 19 credits plus marching band. You may gasp, if you wish. The pressure of this much work is unbelievable. Band takes up at least nine hours a week, and I'm never caught up in my work due to lack of time. That doesn't add much to my concentration ability.

A dittoed copy in my files signals that we had discussed the essay in class, but my memory of the event, perhaps mercifully, has failed. I have no idea what I wrote in the essay's margins, how I addressed the piece (and allowed it to be addressed) in class, what I then diagnosed as its principal strengths and weaknesses, or even what I had hoped to accomplish by the assignment that gave rise to it. I do have a faint idea of what the author might have learned from composing the essay and attending to our criticism of it: that "messed up" needs a hyphen. I suspect that at the time I had no clear idea how to handle this essay, that by instinct more than conviction I took a more-or-less "formalistic" approach.

Today I would take towards that essay, and towards the teaching of writing, what could be called the "epistemic" approach. I would see the activity of composing language as a means of imposing a useful order upon the "blooming, buzzing confusion" (as William James describes it) of one's various and perhaps conflicting sense-impressions—and, at a higher level of cognition, upon one's experiences, thoughts, and bits of factual knowledge. The activity of writing, seen in this light is the activity of making some sense out of an extremely complex set of personal perceptions and experiences of an infinitely complex world. Experimenting in composing with words is experimenting in composing understanding, in composing knowledge. A writer (or other language-user), in a sense, composes the world in which he or she lives. Obviously, the epistemic approach has some distinctive features; what may be less obvious is its close relationship to the more orthodox approaches.

"Epistemic" and Other Ways of Talking about Writing

We can easily see the similarities and differences of epistemic and other approaches by considering an essay like "College Life So Far" in terms of a standard model of discourse. The most convenient model is the familiar "communications triangle" which arranges the four essential elements of all discourse:

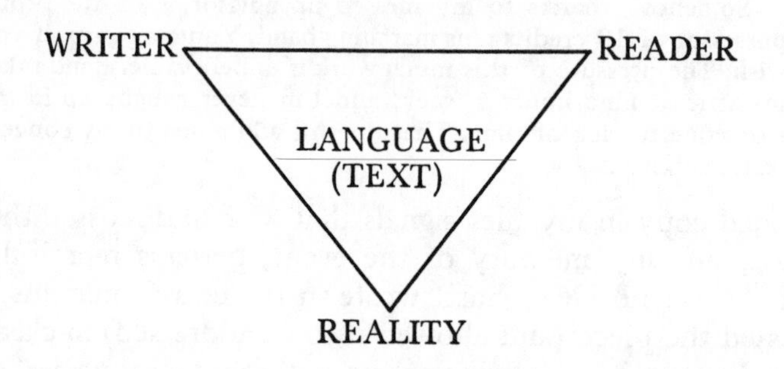

This model is often used to classify theories of discourse (as in M. H. Abrams' *The Mirror and the Lamp*, 1953) or to discuss the aims and modes of discourse (as in James Kinneavy's *A Theory of Discourse*, 1971). It can also serve to classify approaches to teaching writing. Any approach will deal to some extent with all four of the triangle's elements and will emphasize the central element of *language*. The various approaches can be distinguished by their relative emphasis on *writer, reader,* and *reality*. To classify is of course to simplify. In suggesting the essential features of an approach I will have to ignore at first many of its subtleties and the ways in which, if pursued far enough, it begins to intersect with other approaches. But as a beginning, some simple distinctions may be useful.

The formalistic approach focuses mainly on the characteristics of the *language* of the text in itself. This approach is favored by parties as diverse as Strunk and White, James McCrimmon, Richard A. Lanham, and proponents of sentence-combining and T-unit analysis. Formalistic criticism of "College Life So Far" would investigate the essay's style, content, and structure, both in themselves and in relation to conventional rules. It would consider whether or not the two paragraphs should be made into one, whether a concluding sentence is called for, how well the generalizations are supported by specific statements, how complex is the syntax, and, of course, how flawless are the grammar and mechanics. The primary goal of a formalistic course in writing is the production of well-made prose artifacts.

The referential approach sees written *language* primarily as a representation (or even "imitation") of a preexisting and knowable *reality*. This is the approach taken by conventional journalism. It is often taken in technical writing courses or other courses in which writing is combined with the content of another discipline. Referential criticism emphasizes the canons of logic and evidence, the unearthing of "the facts," accuracy, and objectivity. Referential criticism of "College Life So Far" would address questions such as, Is the essay a fair and accurate representation of freshman life at this university? Is the "messed up advisor" in fact to blame for the writer's predicament? Are there any other agencies, besides the six courses and band, that are responsible for the writer's troubles? In a sense, such an approach sees the ideal language as transparent, letting the real nature of things shine through the words clearly and without distortion. The primary goal of a referential course in writing is to enable students to compose those words that exactly fit (and do not obscure) the actual structure of things and events.

The expressive approach, such as that popularized by Ken Macrorie, sees *language* primarily as the expression of the personal perceptions, feelings, and thoughts of the *writer*. Expressive criticism would address questions such as, Does the piece convey a sense of how an individual is perceiving and reacting to experience? Can you understand, care about, empathize with what the writer seems to be feeling? In the case of "College Life So Far," I would give a qualified "yes" to these questions; my students, I think, would give a more enthusiastic "yes." The primary goal of an expressive course in writing is the honest expressing of personal truths.

The rhetorical approach, whether traditional or "New," emphasizes three elements of the communications triangle: *writer, language,* and *reader.* It treats the text as an instrument created by the writer to persuade the reader to undertake the actions or to adopt the attitudes that the writer desires. ("New Rhetoricians" extend the traditional concept of "persuasion" to include "persuasion-to-attitude" or even, as in Kenneth Burke (1965), "ingratiation" or the achieving of "consubstantiality.") Rhetorical criticism of "College Life So Far" would address questions such as, What sort of audience would be most likely to be persuaded (however the term be defined) by this composition? What sorts of appeal is the author making? What sorts of appeal would be most effective upon the actual primary audience of the essay, an English instructor and a class of freshmen and sophomores? By what means could the writer make her audience feel even more sympathy for her plight? The primary goal of a rhetorical course in writing is to increase students' ability to adapt their messages to the values and tastes of their audiences.

These seem to me to be the orthodox approaches to teaching writing: formalistic (emphasizing *language*), referential (emphasizing *language* and *reality*), expressive (emphasizing *writer* and *language*), and rhetorical (emphasizing *writer, language,* and *reader*). The new and less-familiar epistemic approach correspondingly emphasizes *writer, language,* and *reality.* To be sure, in practice and in advanced theory each of these approaches incorporates some elements of the others, yet each does make available a unique combination of insights. I prefer the epistemic approach because the insights it yields are especially useful in dealing with students' writing—useful to teacher and student alike. This will become evident shortly, when we cast an epistemic eye upon "College Life So Far." Before doing so, however, we should understand the epistemic view of writing in general.

Writer, language, and *reality*: the order of these terms is meaningful, for the epistemically-inclined teacher understands that language in a sense comes between the writer's self and objective reality, modifying the former as it gives shape to the latter. The approach assumes what Jerome Bruner concludes, that man "does not respond to a world that exists for direct touching. Nor is he locked in a prison of his own subjectivity. Rather, he represents the world to himself and acts in behalf of or in reaction to his representations. . . . A change in one's conception of the world involves not simply a change in what one encounters but also in how one translates it" (1962, pp. 129, 159). One knows, then, not what is "out there" so much as what one tells one's self is out there by means of symbol-systems paramount among which is natural language. Primarily (though not exclusively) by means of language—thought, spoken, or written—one represents the world to one's self: one translates raw percepts into a coherent experience and transmutes discrete experiences into more abstract sorts of knowledge. By seriously experimenting in manipulating language (on a page, for instance), one experiments in knowing, in understanding the world in different ways.

A corollary is that a way of knowing the world involves a way of conceiving of one's self. As Bruner notes, "Man's image of himself, perforce, is not independent of his image of the world. *Weltanschauung* places limits on and gives shape to *Selbstanschauung*. It is characteristic of man not only that he creates a symbolic world but also that he then becomes its servant by conceiving of his own powers as limited by the powers he sees outside himself" (1962, p. 159). (These words, as we shall see, may be particularly relevant to the plight of the seemingly-helpless author of "College Life So Far.") The way we use language, then, seems not only to reflect but in part to determine what we know, what we can do, and in a sense who we are. To say this is not to deny that phenomena really exist, and not to assert that powerful natural and social forces may be abolished with the sweep of a pen. It is rather to say that our manipulation of language shapes our *conceptions* of the world and of our selves.

Such a view of language and knowledge suggests that writing can be an activity of great importance to the writer. While one in effect composes his or her world by engaging in any sort of language-using, it is by means of writing that one stands to learn the most, for writing is the form of language-using that is slowest, most deliberate, most accessible, most conveniently manipulable, and most permanent. While a person's short-term memory can hold at any time only six or seven "bits" of information, a written paragraph can hold thousands. It can fix them while a writer experiments in connecting bits in various ways, in replacing some with others, in supplementing them with others, in rearranging them, in abstracting and generalizing from them. A writer can tinker with a paragraph for minutes or hours, until it expresses to the writer's satisfaction patterns of cause and effect, evidence and conclusions, interrelationships of data, relevance and irrelevance, denotation and connotation—patterns that establish the "world" in which the writer knows and acts. Such patterns are far too complex and coherent to be created by mere thinking or mere speaking.

Central to the epistemic approach are three closely related propositions: (1) we do not know the world immediately; rather, we *compose* our knowledge by composing language; (2) how we can act depends on what we know, hence on the language with which we make sense of the world; (3) serious experimenting in composing with words is experimenting in knowing in new ways, perhaps better ways. A teacher who assents to these propositions can attain an uncommon but important perspective on student writing.

The author of "College Life So Far," for instance, has composed (with, it appears, very little experimenting) a world in which she is powerless, a victim. It is a world in which other people do things to her (her academic advisor, she asserts, is responsible for her registering for nineteen credits; band "takes up" nine precious hours of her week) or else fail to do things for her ("Very little . . . have [sic] helped me to adjust comfortably"). Her grammar does her no good and some harm. The real trouble with all those passive and copulative verbs is not (as formalists might observe) that they are less "vigorous" than active verbs. The trouble is that these constructions preclude the writer's discovering, exploring, and evaluating ways she might act to improve her situation. What difference might it make to the writer, I would want to ask, were she to rewrite the sixth sentence so that it began, say, "I choose to devote to band . . ."? How else might that sentence begin? Perhaps, "I've been making the mistake of spending . . ."? The writer does not rely on grammar alone to compose this unhappy world. Other verbal structures, for example, the pattern of cause and effect, contribute to this vision. We read that the freshman's inability to concentrate and to complete her work are caused by "unbelievable" pressure and lack of time; that these problems are caused by her having been made the possessor of six courses plus marching band; and that the ultimate cause of all these problems is the personal instability and/or incompetence of a certain "messed up advisor." The *absence* of a third sort of verbal structure likewise assists in this conception of an oppressive world. The writer has *not* composed—at least has not composed here on paper—any verbal connection between her unhappy experiences of the past two months and any previous experiences (direct or vicarious) of the same sort; hence she can find no guidance from the past. Such connecting of different experiences, such designating of phenomena or events as "of a sort" or as relevant to one another in another way, can be achieved only by creating language. In sum, it might be said that the writer's language does not just describe her problem: her language is a real part of her problem.

A "referential" critic might suggest that the essay does not reflect the real structure of things and events at the freshman's college. This is an appealing and convenient way of talking, but, it seems to me, epistemologically unsound. I would say instead that people know the world only by using language to define, organize, and generalize from their limited sense-perceptions (and other language). Even if the world does indeed have a definite structure —a moot point—we can never perceive that structure directly and entirely. We can only experiment in composing verbal models more or less useful in making some sense out of our incredibly complex—yet, it seems, pathetically limited—perceptions.

The trouble with "College Life So Far" is not that it is inaccurate, exactly, but that it is not useful. It is even enslaving. It is a model of a world in which the writer is in no way responsible for any of her problems and in which she is completely powerless to affect what becomes of her. The activity of composing this essay, one can infer, has only reconfirmed and reinforced the writer's victim's-eye view of the world. Were the activity undertaken less hastily and more thoughtfully—were it to involve some serious experimenting with composing specific statements to support generalizations, experimenting with connecting one datum with another, one idea with another, experimenting with composing syntax, experimenting with naming—then the writer might well have come to "see" reality in new and better ways that would suggest some actions she could profitably take. But the nature of the course, the assignment to which the writer responded, her activity of composing, my response to the essay: none of these enabled or even invited the student to find any connections between her writing, her knowing, and her ability to act in a complex and confusing world.

This particular failure to learn and to teach took place some years ago. Today I still fail to enable some of my students to see writing as an activity with profound epistemic and ethical dimensions. But at least I no longer fail to set up the invitation. Nor do I any longer see writing primarily as the production of well-made artifacts (as formalistic pedagogy assumes); nor primarily as a means of self-expression (as expressive pedagogy assumes); nor primarily as a means of describing things accurately (referential pedagogy); nor primarily as a means of communicating more or less persuasively (rhetorical pedagogy). I now see writing, the most deliberate form of language-using, as above all a means of knowing and a means of coming-to-know.

Practitioners of sophisticated versions of the other approaches may in fact agree that language-using is closely related to knowing. They may disagree with "epistemic" teachers mainly over the amount of emphasis the assumption should be given. For example, the formalist Richard A. Lanham concentrates primarily on the crafting of style (that is, diction and syntax); yet Lanham recognizes style's connection to knowledge and identity. "To play with styles," he notes, "is to play with roles, with ways of thinking and, thus, ways of being" (1974, p. 124). Similarly, Kenneth Burke (1951, 1965) and other practitioners of "the New Rhetoric" make use of some central "epistemic" ideas. To persuade, they argue, a writer must first come to understand how—that is, by what sort of language—the audience "sees" things, and then must address the audience (literally) on its own terms. The writer must compose language that enables him or her to conceive of the world as others may see it. "Persuasion" may change the world-view of the writer even more than that of the audience. The predominantly expressive pedagogy of James E. Miller and Stephen Judy also recognizes that language can do more than express preexisting feelings. According to Miller (1973, p. 3), "language must serve the individual, in a fundamental way, in the exploration and discovery of himself and his world."

Such ideas about the fundamental role of language are at least peripheral to other approaches. The epistemic approach moves these ideas from the periphery to the center, and thereby provides a distinctive and meaningful way of discussing writing—and of setting up a writing course.

In a writing class, indeed throughout a university, the principal interest of teachers and students is not in lower-level cognition—in an individual's perceptions and experiences, as such—but in the composing of sophisticated, abstract systems of discourse that select among and connect certain perceptions and experiences, connect them into patterns of relationships so as to produce meaningful guides to future study and future action. Any such system of discourse, whether "chemistry," "history," "literary criticism," or "composition," involves a limited vocabulary (representing a discrete set of concepts) which provides a limited set of categories for classifying observations and experiences and indeed for establishing the sorts of observations that one should make and the types of experiences that one should pursue. Any discourse system involves, as well as a vocabulary, a syntax, a way of relating one concept to another and also a set of conventions for composing larger units of discourse (for example, criteria of evidence and proof, criteria different in rhetoric than in law, different in law than in chemistry). Any discipline can be seen as a system of language, a way of conceiving, talking about, and perhaps making predictions about the world.

At no place in the entire spectrum of knowing—not in complex, abstract, elegant discourse-systems such as advanced science and philosophy; not in the midrange of composing conversation, expository essays, and sophomore lab reports; not in the simplest acts of perceiving and experiencing—do we know anything purely, objectively, immediately. At every level of cognitive activity what we know is bound up with how we use language. "Epistemic" writing courses explore the implications of these conclusions for the activity of expository writing. But the implications extend far beyond the writing class. The insights about the workings of language that students obtain in such a course are applicable not only to standard edited English but to the other, special languages of a university as well. Thus, as William Coles suggests, an epistemic course should "make it possible for a future physicist, say, through his attempts to improve himself in English, to become more responsible to himself as a user of the language of physics" (1974, p. 10).

To make possible such responsible language-using is no easy task. A teacher cannot simply read Bruner to students and then expect immediate improvement in their writing. So an "epistemic" course is usually designed with some care to help students manipulate language in ways that enable them to discover for themselves, and in their own terms, what it means to manipulate language.

The Epistemic Course and its Assignments

Fifteen years ago Richard Ohmann noted what may be the chief reason why, even after English 101, Johnny still can't write: "The trouble with composition courses is less often in the substance of what is taught than in the intellectual framework provided for that substance, and in the motivation offered for mastering it" (1964, p. 22). While the epistemic approach is not the only way to avoid the trouble that Ohmann so acutely describes, it is a very good way. Like most other approaches it teaches the "substance" of invention, organization, and style; however, it addresses these matters always in terms of a well-developed framework of epistemic and pedagogical theory. It offers as motivation the insight that how you compose with words directly affects what you know, what you can do, and in a sense even who you are.

Much of the pedagogical framework was first erected in 1938, with Theodore Baird's famous "English 1-2" at Amherst College. It was further developed by two colleagues and (one might say) students of Baird, Walker Gibson and William E. Coles, Jr. Each of these three has his distinctive style, procedures, and beliefs as do the many other epistemic writing teachers; yet our courses do have enough in common to warrant speaking of a single approach.

The principal goals of the epistemic approach are enabling students to see the extent to which their "worlds" are determined by their language, and helping students to manipulate language—especially written English—in ways conducive to discovery and learning. No conventional textbook or "reader" is used. The principal instructional material is a carefully designed sequence of writing assignments. Most class periods are spent in guided discussions of students' writing, almost always reprinted anonymously. Students write often and much: one or two—in some courses, even three—brief essays a week. These essays are exploratory and personal in nature. In order to encourage honest exploring and risk-taking, the teacher does not usually "correct" or "grade" students' writing. Rather, the teacher writes a few comments or (perhaps more frequently) questions in the attempt to help the writer see and articulate the significance of what he or she has done, or has failed to do. The teacher directs class-discussions with a similar aim. The course progresses over the semester from lesser to greater complexity of idea and statement. The path of the progression is determined by the individual teacher and, to an extent, by the students. The familiar cook's tour through the modes of discourse (or, worse, from the sentence to the paragraph to the theme) is not undertaken.

The most important part of this framework, it seems to me, is the assignments. In an epistemic course, a writing assignment is not just a work-order. It does not order students to produce a composition for the purpose of demonstrating what they have managed to learn about writing. It is designed not to test but to teach—a design that may be worthy of imitation in any writing course. As an epistemically-oriented writing teacher, I can see yet another virtue to the approach, for if language shapes what we know, and if writing is the most considered and manipulable form of language-using, then a well-constructed writing assignment can lead to new knowledge in a very direct way. It can be a heuristic device of impressive power.

A typical "epistemic" assignment calls for some writing activity that students can do with a reasonable degree of competence—describe a block near the campus, say, or tell about a time in which they changed their mind, or describe a church facade before and after reading a treatise on gothic architecture. It also asks a question, in addressing which students must explore the significance, to themselves as writers, of what they have done. This pattern corresponds exactly with the pedagogy Jerome Bruner advocates: any teaching exercise should lead you (the student) to perform a certain task and then "to climb on your own shoulders to be able to look down at what you have just done—and then to represent it to yourself. . . . Our task as teachers is to lead students to develop concepts in order to make sense of the operations they have performed" (1965, pp. 101-102). John Dewey advocated the same process. For him the ideal process of education is the experience of certain activities followed by the "relective review and summarizing" which yield "the net meanings which are the capital stock for dealing with future experiences" (1938, p. 87).

Education (for Dewey, for Bruner, for epistemically-inclined writing teachers, and of course for many others) involves more than increasing the number of data that direct or vicarious experience leads one to know. No less importantly, education involves composing language to connect one datum with another, one experience with another. This establishes patterns by which one can make sense of known data and in terms of which one can discover new data as well. A typical epistemic writing assignment assumes with Dewey that all "teaching and learning [is] a continuous process of reconstruction of experience" (p. 87). It directs students to follow the experience of composing with some "reflective review and summarizing" of what they have been doing.

Many variations are possible within this general form. The following "epistemic" assignments differ significantly in style and specific purpose, and are drawn from very different courses. Assignment 2 of a sequence composed by Walker Gibson, published in his *Seeing and Writing* (1974, p. 36), enacts the typical Gibsonian concern with "seeing":

> Look carefully at the ink blot [on the book's cover] for several minutes. What do you see there? Write out your interpretation so that your reader can see what you see.
>
> (Among the interpretations others have made of this ink blot are: two statues, two birds pecking food, a flower, a butterfly, two pelicans facing each other.)
>
> Now force yourself to make a different interpretation—a different "reading" of these shapes. Write out your new interpretation as before.
>
> Of the several interpretations now before you—yours and those of the other observers—which one do you think is the best one? As you answer that question, what do you mean by "best"?

Assignment 9 of the sequence William Coles describes in *The Plural I* (1978, p. 89) suggests Coles's interest in the composing of personal identity and his inclination (which he shares with Baird, 1952) to let students decide for themselves the perspective from which their "reflective review" will be made:

> "Come, there's no use in crying like that!" said Alice to herself rather sharply. "I advise you to leave off this minute!" She generally gave herself very good advice (though she very seldom followed it), . . . for this curious child was very fond of pretending to be two people.
>
> Lewis Carroll
> *Alice's Adventures in Wonderland*
>
> Describe a situation in which you gave yourself what you consider to be very good advice that you did not follow. Who was there? What was said and done? Did you pretend to be two people? Be sure to explain your answer.

(Coles intends the multiple questions as heuristics; they need not be answered serially or even directly.) My own inclination is to define a little more explicitly than Coles the larger issues that the assignment's initial task raises. Here is Assignment 21 (the fourteenth writing assignment) of my expository writing course:

> Describe a block of Iowa City, creating in your essay the most admirable persona that you can (You define "admirable.")
>
> When you have finished, look back over your essay and try to figure out the principle-of-selection-of-details-to-report that you had been following. (You may or may not have been fully conscious of the principle as you were composing.)
>
> Explain this principle and its relationship, if any, to the quality of your persona.

> Then explain how you would reply to someone who accused you of having been a bad reporter, of having been so concerned with making yourself look good on paper that you weren't true to external reality.

My assignment ends with two requests for "reflective review and summarizing" that directly address the nature and significance of the composing process. Gibson's and Coles's final questions do the same less directly, more subtly. Gibson invites students to confront the role of language in shaping what we see. "The aim here," he explains, "is to cast a little healthy doubt on the assumptions we make about what we see and the World Out There. Seeing is believing?" (1974, p. v). Coles invites students to explore the relationships of language and identity: "The question 'Did you pretend to be two people?,' coming off the quotation from Carroll as it does, . . . seems to me to be a suggestive way of inviting students to deal with the paradox of multiplicity in oneness as a writing problem" (1978, p. 86).

Whatever the nature and style of the final question, it should have three of the characteristics of those above. First, it should call for a generalization of some sort, one proceeding from the writer's "reflective review" of his or her experience in addressing the writing task that the first part of the assignment sets up. Secondly, the question should be directly relevant to the activity of composing with words, so that in addressing it a student stands to learn something about writing. Thirdly, it should be a real question, not a phony one. It should have no single right answer that the teacher knows and the student is supposed to figure out or guess. While it may and perhaps should direct students' thoughts in a certain general direction (e.g., the relationships among selection of details, accuracy, and persona, in my assignment), it should allow and encourage students to make whatever particular discoveries their intellects, inclinations, and experiences in composing lead them to.

The assignments invite the student-writer to engage in the learning process according to Dewey's and Bruner's model. Exactly what is taught, and what learned, depend on the writer as well as on the assignments. "Hence," explains Baird (1952, p. 194), "our assignments are like a scenario rather than a syllabus, an argument of a play rather than the play itself, and to be understood a particular assignment should always be placed in the context of a classroom . . . and read in terms of the student's actual performance. . . . They are stimuli, spring boards, invitations to stand on the edge of an abyss, bear traps, land mines, and often enough they don't work."

An Assignment-Sequence

In an epistemic course, an assignment is part of a sequence of assignments that spiral around a central idea, progressing from relative simplicity to relative complexity of thought and expression. In an initial assignment, the students address a certain issue related to the general theme of the sequence. ("Amateurism and professionalism" is the theme of the sequence Coles describes in *The Plural I*; "seeing and writing" is the theme of Gibson's.) A subsequent assignment provides enough data and questions to complicate the issue in various ways, so that the students must reformulate their positions. Later assignments introduce new data, new questions, new perspectives. At increasingly sophisticated levels the students expand their ideas, refine them, and make new connections between one idea or experience and another. Assignments elicit refining and reconnecting by their thematic relatedness, sometimes by their explicit directions (". . . Now go back and address the question posed by Assignment 2"), and often by their allusiveness, one to another.

One sequence I have developed is the basis of an elective course in expository writing taken mostly by sophomores and juniors of fairly good fluency in written English. With only a little tinkering the sequence, like Coles's and Gibson's, would be appropriate to students of greater or lesser skills. It comprises twenty-four assignments related to the theme of "Good Prose." About sixteen of these call for some out-of-class writing; the number can be varied. As much as possible, I've made every assignment relevant to every other assignment, and I've underscored their relationships by making them highly allusive, one to another. But the spiral is not perfectly seamless; the sequence can be seen as having two parts.

These parts, a dozen assignments each, are complementary. The first group prepares the way by addressing what may be wrong with ill-conceived, sloppy language-using. The second group addresses the positive, creative epistemic aspects of language-using. We begin by addressing what I think is the greatest obstacle to students' seeing writing as a meaningful activity, hence the greatest obstacle to their writing well. This is the habit of cranking out what Coles calls "Themewriting": conglomerations of (at best) half-believed, half-true commonplaces and stock phrases, proclaimed without reservation, more or less well-organized and well-punctuated (often less, but why care?), arranged in the shape of an essay. These safe and meaningless artifacts do nothing for a reader and even less for the writer. So long as students see their own writing as a trick to be pulled–a trick having little connection to the writer's personal thoughts, beliefs, and feelings–no real teaching of writing is likely to occur.

While Themewriting (a.k.a. "Engfish," "Instant Prose," "Black Rot," "Dulness") is a problem recognized by writing teachers of many persuasions, it looks especially bad from an epistemic point-of-view. What is wrong with such fakery, it seems to me, is not only its expressive falsity, its rhetorical ineffectiveness, and often its formal inelegance: by representing the world and their experiences in easy language that they know is far inadequate, Themewriters forswear the possibility of learning anything from their composing and even risk misleading themselves (as false creeds may sound truer the more thay are recited). Beginning the course by examining Themewriting is a good way to start talking about students' writing, to begin chipping away at an obstacle to good writing, to introduce students to an epistemic view of composing, and to prepare the way for the more overtly epistemic assignments which follow.

I begin by passing out and reading aloud a seven-page essay on "The Philosophy and Structure of the Course." It explains what the course will attempt to do and how it will attempt to do it, and advises students of the importance of composing their own connections between one assignment and another. It also urges the students to face squarely and to work at "coming to terms" with any confusion or uncertainty they may feel in addressing the difficult and real questions each assignment poses.

Assignment 1 introduces the central theme of "good prose":

> You have elected to take English 8W:10, presumably, in order to improve your ability to write good prose. Yet what is "good prose" to one person may be "a waste of ink" to another.
>
> In your opinion, as of this time, what is "good prose"? And what exactly is it good for?
>
> And in your own opinion, as of this time, what is "bad prose"? And what's so bad about it, really?
>
> Address these questions in whatever way you can make most meaningful. You will note that no Ultimate Answer is being requested. (Why not, do you suppose?)

This assignment typically results in one or two essays, often from the students with the least-developed writing skills, that contain what look like some genuinely personal opinions. Most of the essays will be hard-core Themewriting, interchangeable imitations of third-rate handbooks. Generally the essayists will fail to enact most of the rules they propound—a fact on which some class-discussions and later assignments can be based. ("Descriptive, colorful words should be used," advised one typical essay, which used none.) The essayists' own opinions, as of this time, will generally be that good prose "conveys" a writer's thoughts with correctness, conciseness, and above all clarity. This foundation will be embellished with exhortations to add concluding paragraphs, to avoid fragments, to get the reader involved, to make transitions clear, and above all to communicate. Bad prose will be defined as the opposite of good prose.

Subsequent assignments invite students to reexamine these platitudes by asking them to come to terms with writing that obeys the prescriptions of clarity, correctness, transitions, and apparent conveyance of thoughts yet nonetheless is insipid or thoroughly unbelievable. For in-class discussions rely at first mainly on essays from a previous class, changing to my students' own essays—reprinted anonymously, of course—when I find some with some praiseworthy spots. I introduce Themewriting as a concept by inviting students to compose some—and then to engage in some Deweyesque "reflective reviewing" of what such composing entails. Assignment 4 paraphrases the basic contentions of the students' initial essays:

> Compose a clear, well-organized, concise, grammatically correct essay—one that efficiently conveys ideas to a reader—on the subject of a good education. Let each statement you make in this essay be true, more or less. Let this essay be in the form of phoniness that you may call "bullshit" or "an English paper," a form that I prefer to call "Themewriting." Note that you are not asked to write anything that you actively believe to be false.
>
> You may (or may not) have composed such a document before. You may possibly even have been rewarded in some way or other for doing so. (What would you say the rewards of such writing are, exactly? Your professor, incidentally, once received a brass-plated trophy and some local fame in exchange for a composition entitled "Optimism: Youth's Most Valuable Asset." As you see it, does one stand to gain anything besides trophies by such writing? What do you think one stands to lose?)
>
> When you have completed this essay on a good education, please address the following questions:

1. Assuming you've followed all the instructions for writing your essay—and I can't imagine any reason you wouldn't be able to —would you call that work an instance of good prose?
2. In your own opinion, as of this time, what *is* good prose?
3. Complete the following definition so that it accurately describes your essay on education and similar works: *"Themewriting:* A sort of prose . . ."

A little later, in Assignment 7, I invite students to compose a genuine essay, not a Themewritten one. It asks that they come to terms with why they are now here at this university. They must also explain why their account should be considered something other than Themewriting. Two or three of the essays I receive will be truly fine; most will be Themewriting in a mock-personal voice with a few specific details thrown in. Probably all of the writers will say that their essay is not themewriting because it is "personal" and because it makes specific statements, not just generalizations.

Assignment 8, begun in class, complicates matters further by asking students to spend no more than ten minutes fleshing out with a few specifics a pair of mock-personal, fake essays on college life. For example:

> . . . These [(a) hot-shot professors with their big reputations / (b) immature TA's] care too much about ________________ and not enough about ________________. For example, in my "____________" class, ________________ ________________________________.
>
> Not that a lot of the courses are worth taking in the first place. I mean, when you're majoring in ____________, like I am, what earthly good do you get out of irrelevant and ____________ [adjective] (but required!) courses such as ____________ and ____________ ?! . . .

This essay's format is a conflation derived from two or three actual essays received for Assignment 7, as is its mate's, which provides for a more positive approach:

> I came to the U. of I. because I want to major in __________, as preparation for a career as ____________. Iowa may not be the best in the country in this field, but its program at least is highly regarded. . . .
>
> Actually, I like it here pretty well. Iowa is big enough ______ ________________, yet small enough ________________ ______. I've gotten to meet a lot of people different from those in my home town (____________________[name]) . . .

In subsequent class-periods we'll try this game with other pieces of student writing, good and bad. Assignment 8 ends by inviting students to articulate, in writing, what conclusions they can make from their experiences in class, and to see what connections they can draw between these fill-in-the-blank representations of the world (and of personal experience) and other representations they have seen or composed in the course.

By mid-semester most students, often to their own surprise, will find themselves and their classmates using written language to create interesting and useful new orders out of their various perceptions, experiences, and ideas. Themewriting will not vanish, but it will decline substantially. No one will have found the Ultimate Answer to the question of what is good prose, but most of us will have discovered that writing can be more than fakery, can be more than avoiding mechanical errors, can even be a means of discovering things one didn't know that one knew, or simply didn't know.

The second half of the sequence, the final twelve assignments, is closely related to the first. Here students explore more directly the epistemic implications of language-using. We explore these not for the sake of general knowledge—this is after all a course in composition, not in philosophy—but for the sake of understanding some of the activities that are involved in composing good prose. Here students confront issues such as what it means to name something; who determines "relevance" (Mother Nature? the individual language-user? someone else?); the basis on which a writer decides what phenomena and events to mention in a composition, and what ones to ignore (and what difference it would make, deciding this one way rather than another); what the term "best" means, as in the best way of organizing material (see Gibson's Assignment 2, above); how such decisions affect persona and apparent accuracy (see my Assignment 21, above); and so on.

Assignment 17, a sort of culmination of all that comes before and a preparation for subsequent assignments, lays the groundwork for examining the activities of naming and of selecting.

> You have discovered that it is possible to talk intelligently about a piece of prose in a number of different ways: its degree of clarity, its degree of honesty, its freedom from error, its diction and syntax, what its writer may have learned in composing it, what a reader might learn in reading it, the nature of the persona, the relationship of one's persona to one's self (as one likes to imagine it), the relationship of one's persona to the ideal self that one would like to become, what the essay invites the

> reader to become, and of course—recall the essays on A Good Education—the relationship of the writer's representation of reality to reality-as-the-reader-understands-it. Eleven ways, at least.
>
> Here are two essays. Talk about them (on paper) in the way(s) that seem most profitable to you. Afterwards, discuss any connections you might see between your way(s) and the others.
>
> (1) A young woman, about twenty-five, sits on a red-white-and-blue bench, eating a sandwich on rye bread, oblivious to the roaring and fuming buses on Clinton Street. She is wearing scarf around her neck, just a hint of makeup and lipstick, and (despite the chill of the afternoon) a short, thin dress, Hershey-bar brown. Next to her sit a paper lunch bag and a copy of Arnold's *Culture and Anarchy*. She gently bites into the sandwich and curls her legs up beneath her.
>
> (2) A girl sits on a dirty wooden bench in the cold afternoon, eating a baloney sandwich. She is about twenty-five, thin, with frizzy hair, not much makeup, and wearing an inexpensive dress. Her hair and dress are the same shade of dull brown. A bus roars by, filthy, dirty, also colored dull brown. The girl crosses her thin legs and bites into the baloney.

In the next few assignments students describe the "world" and the persona each of these paragraphs creates. They attempt substantially different descriptions of the same scene by selecting other combinations of details to report. They can then explore (as in Assignment 21) what the concept of "accuracy" in writing may or may not mean, focus directly on the activity of naming something, and consider what happens when something is named one way rather than another. Here is Assignment 23:

> And no matter what phenomena you select to report, you've got to name them. Think back to the lady on the bench. Consider these issues:
>
> Is she a young woman or a girl (or a lady)?
>
> Is her dress dull brown or Hershey-bar brown?
>
> How about that proteinaceous object in her hand: is it a sandwich on rye bread or is it a baloney sandwich?
>
> Then explain what you mean, exactly, when you use the verb, "is."

The final assignment begins with two quotations from Dewey: "Teaching and learning [are] a continuous process of reconstruction of experience" and, "The value of an experience can be judged only on the ground of what it moves toward and into." It asks students to review the materials they've encountered and the experiences they've undergone in the course, to reflect upon them, and then to assess, in writing, what they've managed to teach themselves about writing. Finally, it asks students to speculate on the uses they might make, in the near future, of what they have learned.

The Rhetoric of Epistemic Teaching

A well-constructed epistemic course is not only theoretically sound: it works in practice. That is to say, the writing of most students improves in many ways over the semester—improves at least moderately and in many cases substantially. Yet it would be foolish to suggest that epistemic pedagogy is the profession's sole and last hope for solving the problem of student illiteracy, or to suggest that an epistemic perspective yields a full and perfect view of the field of human discourse. The approach is not without its limitations.

Its most substantial limitation may be the relatively small amount of attention it is able to pay to the rhetorical aspects of composing, to writing as persuasive communicating. The right-hand side of the communications triangle, the side that contains "READER," is dealt with much less thoroughly than the left. To be sure, an epistemic course is not *a*rhetorical. Students do address their writing to an audience (their professor and classmates) and do respond as an audience to their classmates' writing. Yet it is true that the emphasis is principally on what writing can do for the writer.

But it must be remembered that the epistemic approach is not the only one students will ever have taken. Before most students spend fifteen weeks or so in an epistemic course they will have spent perhaps twelve years in courses based on the assumption that writing is only communication—or, perhaps more accurately, mainly communication, partly the obeying of seemingly arbitrary and seemingly meaningless rules, and partly the romantic or thereapeutic expressing of personal thoughts and feelings. "Good" and "average" students come to college already knowing, though not always enacting, most of the basic techniques of effective communication; they come already knowing most of the rules, including some their professors will never have dreamed of. Some come already "knowing," alas, that it's the (allegedly preexisting) thought or the thing, not the verbal expression, that's important. What students don't know is that they are able to and ought to compose words that have some real importance, some real meaning to themselves and others. And they don't know why they should bother to try to write honestly, let alone why they should spend the real effort it takes to write really well.

I would suggest, then, four reasons why a well-designed epistemic course is likely to make a substantial improvement in students' writing. It is pedagogically sound. It makes available insights that are useful and important. It balances somewhat the excessively formal and rhetorical orientation to writing that students have acquired. And finally, and ironically, it's good rhetoric for persuading our student audience to take the activity of writing seriously. By way of enabling students to see their writing as having a real connection to their knowledge, their freedom, and their selves, an epistemic course addresses the most crucial question about writing that students will ask: "Why bother?"

6 Basic Writing: First Days' Thoughts on Process and Detail

Harvey S. Wiener
CUNY LaGuardia

Right from the start—in the "remedial" or "developmental" course offered to college students—beginners at writing need everything all at once, all the skills in language, form, and structure that each task demands. Yet instructors of beginners know that to try to *teach* everything at once is to be stuck in a quagmire of good intentions. Like a piece of good writing, the basic course needs a design that is clear and logical; and that means that teachers must map out *one* journey to competence (though there might be many) by starting somewhere, by ending somewhere else, by putting some things in and leaving some things out, and by deciding on an order of instruction.

In this chapter I will deal with beginnings, for writers just starting out in any rigorous way, and for the teachers just starting out to teach them. Few of the strategies I will name are original with me—experienced teachers move quickly into the same territories—but I hope to achieve several goals by their treatment here. Simply by stating these strategies I want to suggest first days' thoughts for the teacher new to the still largely uncharted regions of instructing beginners. Also, I want to propose with specific exercises ways to achieve those early goals of instruction. Further, and although this will challenge some stubborn classroom practices, I aim to point out what to omit from the business of the first days in class.

But first consider briefly the kind of student sitting in basic writing courses these days. Mina Shaughnessy in *Errors and Expectations,* defined with searing models the range of idiosyncracies among Open Admissions writers, adding to the writing teacher's vocabulary the indispensable phrase "Basic Writer" (BW). Shaughnessy's remarkable book rebuked forever the longstanding concept of "bonehead English" and redrew lines for respectable courses in writing for the unprepared. For Shaughnessy, BW names the student whose writing shocks through unpredictable error, through twisted, opaque prose. Yet the BW is a student with a logical mind and with reserves of talent for learning.

Although institutions across the country that draw large Open Admissions audiences are concerned with writers similar to these—in degree, if not exactly in kind—the basic skills classroom is by no means peopled only with students labeled as BW's. Shaughnessy (1976, p. 137) herself, with typical insight, wrote: "One school's remedial student may be another's regular or even advanced freshman." That remark, if anything, is more true now as, in a new decade, the "back-to-basics" movement continues to dominate education. The student body is defined by diversity, of course, because in an independent national college and university system, each institution sets its own standards for college literacy, and these are defined by faculty, by students, and by the needs of the community.

In this light, the term *beginning writer* is preferable to *basic writer.* By beginners, I mean those just starting out to learn about writing in any serious way. My term covers Shaughnessy's BW's, certainly; but it also covers writers on campuses like Brown and Penn State and Stanford and Wisconsin, writers without the range and depth of problems noted at the City University of New York and other schools with widely varied student populations, yet writers not viewed as ready for the freshman English course on their campuses.

One of the initial tasks for the instructor of beginning writers is to oversee investigation into the process of writing. Beginners need help in visualizing and in experiencing the stages of creation from the moment a task for writing is defined until the moment the writer submits finished pages for someone to read. This concept of stages is essential for the novice, for whom a word or a sentence set down upon a page with appropriate agony is sacrosanct. As Shaughnessy (1977) points out, the beginner thinks only *amateurs*—never the accomplished writers—change things. Thus, much early work must deal with talk and demonstration of how writers behave.

Beginning with the Process

Beginners need to consider these various stages of writing:

getting an idea to write about (This sometimes means starting from scratch and identifying and narrowing a topic of the writer's own choice and interest; or, it at other times means limiting a topic within the framework of a class assignment.)

determining how to support the idea; whether the writer has sufficient resources to develop it and if not, where to turn for detail

getting the thought down and changing it as it refines itself; adding ideas, combining ideas, ripping open sentences at the beginning, in the middle, and at the end in productive exploration

preparing the thought for someone else to read

Discussion with the class of the steps writers take to carry out a task will reveal a range of surprising misconceptions. "Based on your past experience with courses in school," I always say on the first days, "tell everything you usually do from the time you get a writing assignment until the time you actually hand it in for someone to read." As discussion ensues, I corroborate or question assumptions that arise, and I ask for more information.

"You mean you start writing as soon as you sit down at the kitchen table? What do other people in the class do?"

"You start writing sentences immediately? I start by making a list of everything I can think of."

"What do you do if you get writer's block?"

"What kind of paper and pencil do you use? Do they matter to you? I *must* use long yellow sheets and pencils. Some people work at their rough drafts at the typewriter, but I can't."

Though the work habits revealed in these conversations often make me weak-kneed, I try to honor the subjective responses to this talk of process by acknowledging strong points offered by one student and then another, and by steering the discussion so that, ultimately, I have touched upon the various stages in any written effort. I am not establishing rules here—conditions vary for every task and with every individual—but I am laying out possibilities, increasing awareness. Since process is our theme throughout the semester, there will be lots of opportunities for adjustment and expansion of the concept. At the outset though, I want to impress the class with the idea that despite wide differences, most writers go at their tasks in definable ways.

For the most productive instruction in the writing process,

students need to see what a writer's work looks like at as many stages as possible. That's why it's important for a writing teacher to see himself or herself as a teaching writer, willing to share effort and criticism. Those who have produced articles or books need to put them on display. I bring my own haphazard jottings and outlines to class or I duplicate the pages of a rough draft from my own last written piece and show it to my students. If it's been published, I produce copyedited pages, galley or page proofs, final products.

Little will impress students more than a pock-marked sheet of their teacher's own rough drafts scarred with erasures and cross-outs, with the loops and arrows all writers use to excavate their territory. I look with the class line by line at the starts and stops on a rough draft of my own or of some other writer, at the choices and rejected phrases, at the insertions and excisions. I ask students why they think the writer did what he did on each line and if there is a change *they* might make had they written the piece. Another good idea in this vein is to find a page of rough draft from a well-known writer. Whether it's a Keats ode, a stanza from Eliot, a page from Dickens, a sheet of Lennon's music, I try to show how tentative and exploratory are a writer's thoughts when they reach a page for the first time.

Recent attention to prewriting as an essential area of instruction insists, all for the good certainly, that a writer learn the sundry if often desperate options for stimulating, dislodging, tracking, and developing ideas as he sits alone at the desk amid the anguish of solitary creation. First days' instruction must call attention to those options and must investigate them. Beginners need to know, of course, about thinking through a topic, about getting up from the chair and wandering about if the idea does not come quickly. All writers first *think* about their subjects before doing anything else. If that seems too obvious a point, it is not obvious to beginners who tend to see a writer's spill of words onto the page as magical, inspired, and not at all rooted in careful thought. Thus, the thoughts and their pains, the sudden flashes and their intermittent pleasures are states in the writing process that must be identified for the beginner. Also, those helpful techniques in exploring and developing topics for writing—free association, brainstorming, timed writing, subject trees, scratch or detailed outlines—demand attention too.

Both before they write and while they write, experienced writers advance through prewriting and draft stages at least partially by means of some internal dialogue about their intended thought, about what reveals itself in ink, and about how intention modifies and is modified by the written statement. But that is a conversation beginning writers have rarely practiced. Good instruction, therefore, insists on doing out loud in class what a practiced writer does quietly at home by himself. Instruction in prewriting should attend to external models of awaiting, to private discussions about writing and its process, and to models students can internalize as essential parts of their own procedure. Eventually, guided practice in the informal collection of ideas can move towards the lists or clusters or outlines from which the rough and subsequent drafts grow.

Predictably, this attention puts a high premium upon classroom discussion as an essential element in early writing assignments for beginners. Students need to share experiences which might lead to an effective written piece; and students need to listen to what others in the room say as they grapple with the activity, as they look for and evaluate elements of idea and detail.

For writers to take full advantage of class discussion, each assignment must be crystalline in its requirements. Until much later on in the writer's development, I refrain from assigning the kind of open-ended task that allows completely free range of topic selection. Though it may seem thoughtful to lay a world of choices at the student's feet, I have found that only carefully defined and structured writing assignments (with lots of opportunity for creative activity within those structures) allow incremental learning that can build upon prior achievement and that can be measured, even if only modestly. The more time spent, therefore, in thinking instructions through, in laying out exactly what students must do, the better the results on an assignment.

Once instructions state expectations precisely, the assignment is ready for class discussion. Let's assume that the assignment is description, that the students will describe a place, and that some generalization must control the details offered in support of the topic. Now the class can talk the exercise through. One approach I often use is to put on the chalkboard or overhead projector a list of incomplete sentences that either suggest some opinion about a place or that encourage the student to offer *some* opinion about it. Here are some possibilities.

The noisiest place I know is . . .
A summer place I remember most is . . .
A room that always scared me was . . .
My brother's (sister's) room is . . .
My supermarket is . . .

With a list of at least ten like these I allow some thinking time; and then I go around the room, asking each student to select any sentence and to complete it aloud. After each response I encourage students to explain, extracting detail as I question or—better still—as other students in the class question.

"Why do you say your son's room is messy?"

"Things are all over the place."

"What kinds of things?"

"Oh, a baseball glove and some marbles."

"Just where are they?"

"On the floor near his bed."

"If you were writing about that, what colors and sounds might you add to help someone know the room?"

Having introduced the need for sensory diction, I ask students in the class to help out by suggesting possibilities for concreteness and visual language. As many students as possible in a session should be called on to offer a few sentences of detail. Every member of the class should speak about the assignment in some way. Although many of the students will not write about the subject they have discussed, they do collect ideas from one another; they listen to others coming to grips with the exercise; they discover ways to expand ideas through questioning. It should be made clear that the students will be expected to do all this on their own when they grapple in solitude with a writing task.

This kind of classroom discussion is, of course, only one model. I might simply say, "This week's assignment is the description of a place, one that is particularly lively, one that has some meaning or importance to you. Let's talk about places in your lives that might fit into this category. You might think of a kitchen, your bedroom, a library. Let's have some people in the class talk about places of meaning in their lives." Here, too, students talk, and I encourage and raise questions. "Why do you name your kitchen? Show with words what kind of place it is. What colors are the walls? Are there curtains? What does the table look like? What noises would I hear if I were in your kitchen? What one word would you use to give your overall impression of the place?" Here, impression and evidence, generality and detail, proceed together, interacting and refining each other as the student speaks and the rest of the class listens.

To encourage more independent discussion, I divide the class into groups of three or four. Then I give clear directions: "Each person will describe some important, unforgettable place to the rest of the people in the group. One person as secretary will take notes as others talk; the rest of the group will ask questions which will lead to sharp sensory pictures. You might want to ask about location, color, sound, action, people. Don't take more than a couple of minutes with each speaker. After each group is finished, the secretary will describe briefly what was said for the rest of the class. And we'll all listen for the clearest description."

These are only suggestions; the point is to bring the class to such a pitch of interest and excitement about the topic through sharing ideas that these ideas will spill over onto a page once formal writing begins. A second point, of course, is to supervise activities—thinking through the topic, asking questions about it, searching for detail, weighing the validity of a generalization—that the inexperienced writer can practice alone before writing.

Another essential exercise in prewriting for beginners is examining and analyzing student essays written in response to the assignment by others in the past. After explaining an essay and after supervising class discussion, an instructor can provide through student models tangible examples of writing that meets the goals for the activity. But the examination of models must be more than someone reading and others merely listening, with benign but superficial and unconstructive comments afterwards. When considering a model, students must be clear about why they are considering it. Pointed questions asked beforehand can direct concentration: "Listen to this description by Lawrence Skibicki. Afterwards, be prepared to answer these questions: What is the topic statement? Which sensory appeal to sound did you find most original? What transitions help the reader move from thought to thought?" Without asking too many questions, instructors can focus upon important concerns awaiting the writer on the essay assignment.

For beginning writers, models from students, as opposed to professionals, have special value. A favorite among teachers, perhaps, the professional model is at times more a threat than an opportunity for emulation. Models by students say something important to the novice: "Here is a piece written a while back by someone in a class like this one. It may be better than your writing now, but it's not something you cannot reach if you apply the principles we've been discussing."

I have concentrated so far upon two important dimensions of the writing process. First, I have pointed to the kind of exposure to prewriting strategies required by beginners on the first day or two of the course. That exposure includes the various stages through which writing generally proceeds and the various pre-writing options available for writers to stimulate invention and the successive production of drafts. I have also proposed that pre-writing for early assignments should involve active discussion as models for dialogues beginners can internalize and can use when they face a writing challenge unassisted. In a sense this second suggestion gets me a bit ahead of myself. Before offering formal essay exercises, a course for beginners should deal with some critical skills in language. I want neither to neglect them nor to set them out of place.

Most teachers assert the priority of language skills right from the start of the term. Unfortunately, however, in an attempt to help beginners develop competence and facility with language many beginning instructors attend to correctness as the first and major task. They turn exclusively and almost by instinct to intensive work in grammar and the structure of language. Starting the term off with instruction in parts of speech, followed by drill aimed at error, is wrong for many reasons but especially because it is a miscue. It says that the first order of business in learning to write is building a command over systems for describing and using language instead of building a command over language itself. Basic writing courses I have examined on many campuses are still dark forests of nouns and verbs and adjective clauses, with students as hunters circling the prey and fixing it with names. This is true despite the general and longstanding disfavor of such approaches among theoreticians in writing instruction. Erika Lindemann in a fine book soon to be published by Oxford University Press sums it up crisply:

> We cannot improve our student's writing abilities if we focus exclusively on the code, on grammar or on the surface features of the written product. Students who cannot find anything to say, even though they write not the first misspelled word, can be as ineffective as communicators as students who have brilliant ideas but ignore the reader's need to have them presented in reasonably punctuated sentences.

Details

For effective communication, students should work closer to the writer's craft by focusing as soon as possible upon the nature and invention of precise language and detail instead of upon labeling subjects, verbs, and objects. Few skills demanded from writers are as important as skill in the use of detail. To expand an observation by means of concrete diction is one of the hallmarks of clear, persuasive writing; and the absence of specific detail can easily brand a written effort as superficial.

Though instruction in the use of detail is important for all students, teaching novice writers about it is a special challenge. Students must, of course, learn to marshal evidence in support of an idea. But they must first learn how to construct that evidence with language, how to turn perception, idea, and observation into words, how to use words to convey exactly the information the writer wishes them to convey. Beginners must also expand an often limited supply of language suitable for standard expression, if they are to report accurately the sensory data the mind and body program instinctively. Instruction in detail starts on the most basic levels of language awareness, vocabulary acquisition and sharing. Classroom activities need to focus upon words as carriers of precise information.

Because the beginner's main disadvantages in vocabulary are both inability to remember forms and definitions of words *and* a lack of judgment in using words appropriately, Shaughnessy (1977) suggests three kinds of learning when the student approaches vocabulary: learning about words, learning words, learning a sensitivity to words.

It is in her last category where I believe early course instruction is essential and where it lays a foundation upon which a term's program can build productively. Teachers cannot work too soon nor too much with, for example, the notions of general and specific language, in order to give students a feel for the range of meanings words allow. A study of groups that move from general to specific is highly productive:

1. food	1. plant
2. meat	2. herb
3. steak	3. flower
4. sirloin	4. tulip

How do meanings change from 1 to 2 to 3 to 4? What advantages serve a writer using 4 instead of 1, 2, or 3? Students should examine lists of words, supplying specific ones for general ones, arranging them in their order of specificity.

Along with distinctions in language specificity, beginners also need an understanding of denotation and connotation; by substituting for a key word in a sentence another with similar definition but with different connotation, instructors can offer illustrations:

> The *doctor* treated my mother.
> The *physician* treated my mother.
> The *specialist* treated my mother.

How does the meaning of the sentences vary with the change in word?

With the need established for specific language and for awareness of shades of meaning, the beginner's attention should turn to concrete sensory language and imagery. Probing the close-by physical environment first, beginners must learn, as a starting point for control over detail, how to generate language that evokes the senses. Teachers must explain the way the mind acquires data through the senses and the way a good writer attempts to turn his perceptions into language that arouses the reader's imagination. This calls for a review of the storehouse of words that name sensations: *hot, rough, bumpy* for touch; *smoky, sweet, dusty* for smell; verbs like *clatter, thud* and *whisper* for sound; or *plunge, hobble, creep* for actions—and innumerable others. Beginners will see easily how colors establish immediate visual recognition, how words for sounds fill the language. Lists of sense words organized into appropriate categories help expand working vocabulary.

Once writers investigate and experiment with sensory language they need to develop skill at imagery, the sustained sensory pictures that capture time. A good beginning asks students to compare words with images of different levels of concreteness, at first without attention to complete sentences:

1. a car
2. a green Ford
3. a green Ford rattling to a stop

How has the writer in 3 achieved a higher level of concreteness than in 1 or 2? What word in 3 adds color? Which adds sound? What words could the class substitute for the color word, the sound word, even for the highly specific noun? Experiment with turning the image in 3 into sentences that paint even more exact pictures:

4. At dawn a rattling green Ford sputtered through the snow on High Street.
5. At a red light on Broadway and Eighth, a rattling green Ford screeched to a halt last night.

Which do readers prefer—3, 4, or 5? Why? What details in 4 and 5 create different pictures despite similarity of subjects?

Students can suggest their own images for familiar objects and can then build those images into full sentences. (Here is a means of assessing early on the class's sentence sense without a formal lesson in grammar.) When building sentences, students should draw upon the lists of sense words. Verbs that state specific actions are of particular value in these activities. After examining sentences with vague verbs like *walk* and *is* students can substitute strong verbs that name actions clearly. Another productive exercise asks the class to examine a short paragraph alive with sensory language but with all the sense words removed, blanks in their places. Under each blank a word like *sound* or *color* or *touch* signals the kind of sensory appeal the writer aimed for; students then insert their own words. Afterwards the two samples—student's and original—laid side by side provide valuable insights into word choice and individual creativity.

After exploration and practice of sensory language some beginners develop problems with overmodification. Frequently a student learning about sensory language will fill his prose with adjectives. How could the class change this—*The tall, thin-legged, nervous, red-haired woman rushed away*—so that the adjectives do not cluster before the noun? Sometimes a different, more expansive, structure provides flexibility; sometimes a more specific noun will do it. An alternative like this one might better serve the writer: *As the wind blew her red hair, a tall woman rushed away nervously, her thin legs wobbling.* Practice like this in converting the smothered-noun image lays foundations for later activities in sentence expansion and embedding, foundations that require no extensive grammatical brickwork.

Often efforts at imagery provide modifiers with few pictorial qualities. No matter how clear the instructions, writers learning about detail are often more apt to *tell* than to *describe.* As a result, work in distinguishing differences in phrases like these is essential:

1. a *cute* girl with a *pleasant* smile
2. a *blonde* girl with *freckles* and with an *open-mouthed* smile

Though *cute* and *pleasant* aim for pictures, they miss the mark. The image they are intended to draw is not yet transformed from the writer's mind into visual language. Just what does *cute* mean to members of the class? Pleasant? Registering those words, would student's minds have called up the same images that appear in 2?

Almost certainly not, and that provides another essential key to the craft of the writer: unless he or she describes an observation precisely, adjectives that interpret can frequently set a reader's resultant images at odds with the writer's. Only by inference from the verbal picture should a reader know that a child is cute or that her smile is pleasant.

As if excessive use of interpretive adjectives were not problem enough, the beginning writer's supply of those adjectives is sorely limited to a group noted for their vagueness: *good, nice, cute, bad, higher, lower, less, worse, many, a lot, much, hard, easy*. By means of exercises in word options, in careful observation, and in the recording of observed phenomena through sensory language, students can develop a trust in their own sensory perceptions. The writing of clear, precise images is the heart of the matter, of course. It is a skill that most students can learn, even if they demonstrate their skills only intermittently at first. Once secure in the construction of sensory detail, students can then learn to control it in a paragraph or an essay, eliminating images that do not pertain to an established generalization.

Not always, but often in the beginner's movement toward command over concrete diction there follows a sequence starting with opinions not substantiated by detail, to opinions backed up with details that are really editorial, to, finally, opinions rooted in original observation. Despite a student's ability to write images in classroom exercises, learning to incorporate imagery as an element of supporting detail is a slow process. A set of sentences like 1, 2, and 3 following, for example, can help to encourage expansion:

1. The city has many problems. One problem is the bad transportation. It's terrible. Another problem is sanitation . . . .

While keeping in mind what has been learned about specific language, supporting detail, and imagery, the student, revising, generates sentences such as the following which seem to meet the request for detail:

2. The city has many problems. One problem is the subways. The trains are dirty and unpleasant. The floors are filthy. Another problem is . . .

Now that's an improvement. Naming *subway* and *trains*, the writer moves into the territory of concreteness. *Dirty, filthy, unpleasant*—although they are too general to evoke a picture and are examples more of telling than of showing—take the writer somewhat beyond the realm of unsupported assertion that appears in 1. Still, no clear details draw the reader into the writer's mind. Review, more work on expanding pictures with sense words, repeated instructions to individualize a scene can in time yield sentences like 3 following, much more consistent with the goals of writing rich in supporting detail:

> 3. The city has many problems. One problem is the subways, which are dirty and unpleasant. Yesterday on the Flushing local cigarette butts and crumpled pages of *The Daily News* lay everywhere. Streaks of black and yellow paint covered the windows. On the only empty seat in the car sat a paper bag wet from cola that dripped to a brown puddle on the floor.

It takes a while to bring a beginning writer as far as the few consecutive sentences in 3. But to view those in 2 as a good enough end point for achievement is no service to the beginning writer. True, there is an attempt at presenting sensory data; but it is too insubstantial to be accepted as a finished effort.

After instruction in the writing process and in the use of detail, the course can proceed to the traditional rhetorical mode, starting with paragraphs or description and narration. Throughout the course writers will work towards developing their skills in the use of detail. As they learn to convey observations in the language of sound, color, action, smell, taste, and touch, students can move to a higher and higher level of concreteness. As instruction develops, they can learn to offer other kinds of details—statistics, cases, and other forms of reliable testimony—but these skills are often hard to treat adequately within the initial course given the range of skills that need developing.

For beginners, then—for teacher and student—process and detail are springboards for reliable development during the course. These basic elements need investigation before anything else, certainly before issues of correctness demand attention. It is only when beginning writers are convinced that they have something meaningful to say and that they can develop their sentences through a series of exploratory stages—only then do efforts with the conventions of written language sound a responsive chord among students just learning to take writing seriously.

Portions of this essay will appear in *The Writing Room: A Resource Book for Teachers of English*, New York: Oxford University Press, forthcoming.

7 The Writing Conference: A One-to-One Conversation

Thomas A. Carnicelli
University of New Hampshire

The conference method of teaching writing has become increasingly known and accepted in recent years. A conference may be as short as thirty seconds, or as long as the two parties wish to talk. It may be held in a corner of a classroom, in a hallway, or cafeteria. It may be conducted by telephone. But all the forms have the same essential feature: only two parties, a teacher and a student, not a teacher and a class. The conversation between these two parties, rather than statements or written comments by only one, is the strength of the conference method.

The conference method is regularly discussed at conferences and workshops and in the professional literature, where testimonials to its effectiveness have become quite common. Rather than simply adding my own testimony to the list, I've sought to provide evidence from a new, and perhaps more objective, source. I've collected the opinions of the other parties in the writing conference, the students themselves.

The Freshman English program at the University of New Hampshire has relied on the conference method for the past eight years. Each student has a weekly, or bi-weekly, conference throughout a fifteen-week semester. At the end of the semester, each course section is evaluated by the students on a form which requires detailed written comments, not mere check marks. In preparing this chapter, I have read all the student comments from the ninety-two sections offered in the 1977-8 academic year. Since an average of twenty out of the twenty-six students per section actually filled out the form, I have examined approximately 1,800 student responses to conference teaching. This sample was more than large enough to provide a clear and consistent picture. I did not perform a statistical analysis of this material, but simply recorded typical and recurring comments. To compensate for my own bias, I made a special effort to record any negative comments.

Negative comments were, however, comparatively rare. The great majority of the students liked the conference method, and felt they had learned a great deal from it. These student comments, both positive and negative, provide unusually clear insights into why the conference method works and how it can be used to best advantage. To supplement the discussion of the student responses to conference teaching, I present a transcript of a fairly typical student conference—one which resulted in a satisfactory paper. Lest this example of conference teaching seem "too good to be true," I also present a transcript and analysis of a New Hampshire conference that failed. Conferences are not a panacea. Conference teachers fail every day, just like any other kind of teacher. Yet our failures can be as instructive as our successes.

A Definition of the Conference Method

It's impossible to discuss the individual conference in isolation. Conferences are parts of courses; they work better in some types of courses than in others. When I refer to the conference method, I mean the use of conferences within a course based on certain teaching principles. These principles are essential to the most effective use of the conference itself.

The first principle is that writing should be taught as a process. For my purpose here, I'll simply use the well-known definition of the writing process as three stages: prewriting, writing, and rewriting. Traditional writing instruction usually stresses only the writing stage: the student is given a topic and writes a first draft; the teacher grades the draft, then assigns another topic. There is little or no time for prewriting or rewriting. Only the paper, the product, receives the teacher's attention. Teachers who use a process approach stress all three stages, with special emphasis on the third. In a process approach, student papers are treated as drafts, as papers-in-process. Revisions are counted as new papers, and students are encouraged to work on the same paper for several weeks, rather than being forced to drop a promising subject and dig up a new one. Weekly papers are not graded. Grading is done at the end of the semester, and is based on several revised papers of the student's own choice.

Conferences are especially effective in a process approach because they occur when the student needs and appreciates the teacher's help. If the student "can't think of anything to write about," a prewriting conference can help identify some promising subjects. If the student has found a decent subject but has written a dead-end draft, a conference can suggest new questions to ask, new possibilities to explore. Students are highly receptive to help in mid-process because it responds to problems they have actually encountered, not ones they may possibly encounter, and it allows them to work on those problems before submitting the paper for a grade. A conference in mid-process is immediately useful. In contrast, a conference after a paper has been graded is an autopsy; it dwells on past failures, not future possibilities, and it provides advice to be used in some nebulous "next time." A student sitting there staring at a poor grade will not be very receptive to that advice, may not even hear it. Conferences after grading may have some value, but only in a process approach can the full value of the conference be realized.

Even if a conference is offered at the right time in the writing process, it may not be effective if the teacher does not follow the second essential teaching principle: "First things first." A conference teacher must have a reasonable set of teaching priorities in responding to student papers. A student's first draft is likely to have a multitude of problems, everything from confused ideas to comma splices. If the teacher tries to address all of them in a single conference, the student will end up confused and discouraged. The conference will be far more useful if the teacher focusses on one or two of the most important matters and makes sure the student understands them. Other problems can always be discussed in subsequent conferences if they are still present in the revised drafts.

The priorities I use and recommend are borrowed almost wholesale from Roger Garrison (1974): content (ideas and information), point of view (purpose, persona, audience), organization, style (diction and syntax), and mechanics (grammar and punctuation). Content and point of view are my "first things" because they seem to me the basic elements of writing itself, which I define as someone (persona) communicating something (content) to someone else (audience) for some reason (purpose). I address the other elements on my list only after I feel the basic problems of content and point of view in a paper have been adequately dealt with. I might, for instance, see the same paper two or three times before paying much attention to style or grammar. A full defense of my particular set of priorities is unnecessary here. My point is simply that a conference teacher must develop a set of priorities based on a reasonable understanding of what writing is. Not even conferences will help the teacher who treats grammar as more important than content.

Conferences, a process approach, and a reasonable set of priorities—that is my full definition of the conference method. Courses may vary widely in specific details, but, if they adhere to this definition, they are using the same basic method of teaching writing.

There are two common formats for writing courses based on the conference method. One, which might be called the "short conference" or "conference only" format, is best exemplified in Garrison's freshman course. In this course, conferences are everything. After the first week or so, class meetings are abolished and the classroom becomes a writing workshop, where the teacher holds conferences in one corner while the other students sit and write. Papers are kept short—no more than six or seven paragraphs. Conferences are also short, running from three to five minutes on the average. In fact, Garrison sometimes manages to hold up to twenty conferences in a fifty-minute class hour. He achieves this amazing pace because he treats only one problem per conference and he sees the same paper so often—sometimes in four or five drafts—that he can respond to it very quickly. In essence, Garrison's format relies on short papers and on short and frequent conferences to teach students to write.

This format is the most feasible way to use conferences when a teacher has a large number of students and no practical way to meet with them outside of class hours. It has been used successfully in many two-year colleges, and is especially suited to community colleges where many of the students live off-campus and hold full-time jobs. It has also been used successfully in high schools, although it is no mean feat for a teacher to keep a roomful of young students quiet while conferring with individuals in a corner.

Where the teaching load is not so heavy and where students are readily available outside of class hours, another, less Spartan format can be used. The freshman course at New Hampshire is a convenient example. Conferences are the most important part of the course, but they are not the entire course. Classes do meet regularly, although often one of the class hours is used for conferences. Classes are used to critique student papers, to do certain writing exercises, and to discuss writing in general. Papers and conferences are both considerably longer than in Garrison's format. Students are required to write five pages a week, and to attend a fifteen to twenty minute conference at least every other week. Enough extra time is set aside so that every student may have a conference every week, and many choose to do so. Conferences are usually held in the teacher's office. Essentially, this format relies on longer papers, longer but less frequent conferences, and on classes to teach students to write.

I hold no brief for one format against the other. While I happen to enjoy classes and would hate to give them up, I believe they are far less important than conferences in teaching writing. If a teaching situation requires a choice between classes and conferences, classes should definitely go. Whether short papers combined with short, frequent conferences are more effective than longer papers and longer, less frequent conferences is not for me to say. Teaching conditions and personal temperament should determine which format a given teacher should use. Both have proven successful for teachers who have used them. They are, after all, adaptations of the same teaching method, not two separate methods. Virtually everything I say about conferences at New Hampshire will apply equally well to conferences in the Garrison format.

A Rationale for the Conference Method

There are many good reasons for using the conference method. Some were readily apparent to the students in my study. Others are best understood and appreciated by teachers. I have grouped them all together under five main headings.

Individualized instruction in writing is more effective than group instruction. The individual nature of conference instruction is what impressed the students in my study the most. While I wasn't seeking to make statistical analysis of the student responses, one statistic was easy to compile: not one of the 1,800 students found classes as useful as conferences. Some of the students put the matter quite bluntly. "Without conferences, the course would be meaningless." "Conferences are helpful, but class is a waste of time." Of course, if the classes were really bad, such comments don't say too much for the conferences. Most students found at least some value in their classes, but even those who liked their classes the most found them less useful than the conferences. "Although valuable information was disseminated during class, I learned about *my* writing in my biweekly conferences." "As far as the classroom is concerned, much is learned about general writing practice, but as far as individual writing is concerned, the conference *cannot* be replaced. Here is where the most learning takes place."

This type of comment appeared again and again. While many different activities are used in our classes, not one was singled out as especially helpful, not even class discussions of student papers—by far our most common classroom activity. Students seemed to perceive all class activities as devoted to "writing in general" and found none of them directly relevant to their individual writing problems. These responses may be disheartening, but they are not surprising, at least to me. After years of laboring to design useful and interesting writing classes, I'm under no great illusions about what classes can accomplish in a writing course. Writing classes can be moderately useful, perhaps more useful than students immediately realize, but they are certainly not essential. Learning to write is a uniquely personal process; students learn to do it primarily by working on their own papers.

The strictly psychological value of individual writing conferences was also apparent in the student comments. A number of students expressed deep insecurity about themselves as writers and appreciated the privacy of the conference. "You're never afraid of being embarrassed because it's between her and yourself." "Here you can discuss your writing alone with the teacher. You don't have to fear criticism from other students." Most students were impressed by the personal interest their teachers showed toward them in conference. "The conferences give me a sense of individuality, that my paper means something to someone other than myself." Such advantages could be derived from individual conferences in any course, but they are particularly important in a beginning writing course, where so many students have such low opinions of their own abilities.

The teacher can make a more effective response to the paper in an oral conference than in written comments. A teacher who reads papers at home and relies on written comments is working in a vacuum. If the task were simply to assign a grade, this practice would be sufficient; but, if the task is to help the student revise the paper, the teacher can benefit greatly from the student's actual presence.

A conference is far more effective than written comments as a way of communicating with students. The tongue is faster, if not mightier, than the pen. It is possible for a teacher to make more comments in a conference than in an equal amount of time spent writing. It is easier and more efficient to talk about complex problems than it is to write about them. That's why teachers give up and write "See me" on certain papers. Written comments serve very well for correcting small points of grammar or style, but it is difficult to clarify a large problem of content or point of view without talking to the student. The presence of the student allows the teacher to tailor a response to the student's needs. A point that might take five minutes of painstaking writing to explain can be dismissed in ten seconds if it's apparent that the student fully understands it. A comment that might seem obvious to the teacher may require a more detailed explanation than could have been anticipated. Finally, the presence of the student enables the teacher to be more tactful, or more forceful, as the student's attitude warrants. The conference teacher can better judge how much to say, and how to say it.

A teacher reading a paper at home is deprived of two invaluable resources: the student's information and the student's opinions. A conference teacher can use these resources to respond more accurately to the paper. Students come to conference with an enormous amount of information about their papers. They know, more or less, what they were trying to accomplish in the paper. They know the problems they encountered in writing it. They know what they meant in specific words and sentences. They know other ideas and facts about the subject that they couldn't manage to fit in. All of this information can be immensely useful to the teacher in diagnosing the paper and in suggesting new possibilities or entirely new topics. The student's opinions of the paper are equally valuable in shaping the teacher's response to it. The student provides another mind, another perspective on the paper. The very process of discussing the paper with the student can help the teacher understand it better. If the discussion turns up significant disagreements, so much the better. A good argument from the student can help the teacher clarify or modify an inadequate response.

Not surprisingly, this last advantage of the conference was not apparent to the students in my study. Students assume that the teacher, the expert, always knows exactly what to do with a paper after reading it. They have not been trained to believe that they can actually contribute to the teacher's understanding of their work. They can, and do, contribute in conferences, whether they realize it or not.

The student can learn more from an oral response than from written comments. For most students, a writing conference is a new experience. They've never discussed their writing with a teacher before. They've simply received written "corrections," usually in red ink. Apart from the special demerits of the red ink approach, which is universally detested by students, written comments in general have serious disadvantages when compared to criticism given orally. Written comments are more impersonal. They are often more difficult to understand. Most importantly, they are strictly one-way communication; the student has no immediate chance to question or disagree.

Students are more receptive to criticism given orally because they can appreciate the spirit in which it is offered. They can sense the teacher's support and concern, and realize that even negative comments are intended to be constructive. It is difficult for a teacher to demonstrate the same degree of personal concern in written comments alone. Even the most tactfully phrased written comment may seem destructive to a beginning writer.

Written comments can be ambiguous or confusing to students. If students cannot understand a teacher's response, they may simply ignore it, or else follow it without knowing why any change is necessary. In a conference, of course, this problem can be outflanked. If the teacher's response is unclear, the student can simply ask for an explanation. Many students in my study stated that the conference helped them understand the teacher's response to their writing. "During conference, she helps me find a better way to write it so that we understand why it should be done, not just that it should be changed." Some of the teachers here write comments on papers and return them prior to the conference—a practice I don't much like, for reasons that should be apparent. The comments of some of their students say a great deal about the limitations of written criticism. "The instructor can comment all he wants, but the corrections don't come to life until he shows you exactly what he means in conference." "The criticism has been constructive. It helped a great deal when I could see what he meant by going to conferences. If I had just read the comments without explanation, I might have felt the criticism was destructive."

A student who has worked long and hard on a paper needs the chance to defend it. Not all students are willing to take that chance, but the conference makes it readily available. A number of students in my study praised the opportunity to "disagree" or "argue" with the teacher. Most saw argument as a kind of adversary proceeding, leading to a compromise. "Sometimes her criticism hasn't been correct, but then when the problem was discussed we came to a compromise. I'm willing to stick up for my writing, and if she disagrees, I'll argue my point." While teachers tend to take a less pugnacious view of argument, seeing it more as a joint opportunity than a battle, this difference in attitude has no practical effect. If the student "wins" the argument, the teacher "wins," too. The student gains confidence as a writer and self-critic, as well as respect for the writing course itself. The teacher gains a better insight into the paper and, more importantly, the student's active involvement in the process of criticism.

Written comments do have their uses, even in the conference method. They're more permanent than oral comments, not dependent on the vagaries of memory. Several students in the study commented on how difficult it was to remember what went on in conference. "The criticism was worthwhile, but I wish I had written down the suggestions—there just isn't time to do so in conference." There's a simple solution to this problem. Either the teacher or the student can make notes on the paper during the conference. Students don't mind marks on their papers—if they have had a hand in making them.

Conferences can promote self-learning. When the teacher's response is given first, whether orally or in writing, the student is put in a reactive position. Even though the student may ask questions and raise objections, the teacher's response usually determines the focus of the conference. This is a useful type of conference, and it may be the most effective in many teaching situations; yet it does not fully exploit the greatest single advantage of the conference method. Conferences are an ideal way to promote self-sufficiency and self-learning in students. To encourage their students to make fully independent judgments, some teachers prefer not to give any response to the paper until after the student has responded first. They try to make the student's response, not their own, the focus of the conference.

This is the most common type of conference at New Hampshire, and the students in the study provided some good descriptions of it. The teacher attempts, through questioning, to lead the student to make some conclusions about the paper. "He concentrated on my reaction to the paper. Just with gentle hints, I was surprised at what mistakes I saw myself." The teacher states an opinion directly only after the student has done so, or at least tried to do so. "She gets me to criticize it first, which usually covers most of her criticisms, and then she adds on." The teacher's opinion is offered in response to the student's and serves either to confirm it or suggest that it be modified. The student may accept the teacher's opinion, reject it, or work out a combination of the two views. The ultimate decision of what to do with the paper is left to the student. "She'll ask you what *you* think should be done, give her opinion on how to revise the paper, and then we work out a compromise on what should be done. If you don't like her way, you can do it your own way without being degraded."

Although this approach is quite different from traditional writing instruction, most students in my study understood it and appreciated its value. Most of them expressed a clear willingness to accept some responsibility for their own learning. Some even acknowledged that the teacher had a right to refuse to help them if they refused to help themselves. "She made us think about why we were writing the way we were and how to correct it. She did not always offer ways of changing our papers if we did not give any ideas or suggestions. If we did, she was very helpful." "She is always willing to give suggestions for a new way to present a paper as long as we show that we are thinking too. She's not about to do all the work for us."

The conference method is the most efficient use of the teacher's time. The conference method is not only the most effective way to teach writing, it is also the most efficient. It can increase a teacher's effectiveness with no increase in teaching time. In some formats, it can increase the teacher's effectiveness while actually decreasing the amount of teaching time.

The Garrison format requires the least amount of the teacher's time, since the teacher has no classes to prepare for. If, as Garrison insists, the teacher reads the papers only in conference, then the task of reading papers at home is also dispensed with. Garrison recommends some tasks for the teacher in addition to conferring during class hours—notably, designing specific writing projects or assignments that students may choose to perform. Still, the fact remains that, for the teacher who has the skill and energy to use it, the Garrison format is the least time-consuming way of teaching writing effectively.

While the New Hampshire format requires more time than Garrison's, it is no more time-consuming than traditional writing instruction, provided the teacher reads the papers for the first time in conference. It is the task of reading papers at home that is the real time-killer in traditional course formats. After twenty years of experience, I still cannot read a five-page paper and make a reasonably detailed written response to it in much less than twenty minutes. Given the same paper and a twenty-minute conference, I can accomplish a great deal more, without using any more time. In fact, I even gain some time: nights and weekends. At the end of a full day of conferences, I may be exhausted, but at least I don't have a stack of papers to take home with me.

I've put the argument from efficiency last because educational considerations ought to precede pragmatic ones. I also would not like to advertise the efficiency of the conference method too boldly, lest pragmatic administrators see it as a way to increase teaching loads. The teaching loads of most writing teachers are already too heavy. In fact, those excessive teaching loads are the main reason why many beleaguered writing teachers don't believe the conference method is feasible for them. A teacher who has five sections of composition and 175 students a semester is likely to regard the idea of individual conferences as hopelessly impractical. I maintain, though, that conference teaching can be practical in such a situation, that it may, in fact, be the best way to cope with such outrageous teaching conditions. A teacher who is willing to give up classes and written comments on student papers—no great losses, educationally—can teach effectively by individual conference even with large numbers of students. The choice is up to the individual teacher, and there really is a choice. Conference teaching is a practical option, not an impossible ideal.

The Conference Teacher's Role

Given the value of the conference method, what can a teacher do to put it to best use? To answer this question, I want to define the conference teacher's role more clearly. There are, I believe, six essential tasks that a conference teacher must perform.

The teacher should read the paper carefully. This would be a truism unworthy of comment, except for the fact that it leads directly to one of the major issues in conference teaching. Should the teacher read the paper beforehand or read it for the first time in conference? Most of the recent articles advocate inconference reading. I recommend it, too, but the issue is not a simple one.

The basic question is, of course, whether inconference reading allows the teacher to make an accurate and thorough response to the paper. Several students in my study found the practice unsatisfactory. "I do not think the teacher is prepared enough to criticize." One comment was unusually detailed and, I think, perceptive. "Sometimes she will read my paper for the first time during the conference and will merely skim read it. This is not good evaluation because in these instances I find her criticisms concern words or small phrases that she happens to come across rather than the paper in general." This kind of random and superficial sniping is always a danger. Nevertheless, inconference reading can be extremely effective after a teacher has learned how to use it.

For a teacher new to the conference method, inconference reading is usually too difficult, too threatening. At New Hampshire, only a few brave souls attempt it from day one. Most new teachers here work into it gradually. For the first half or two-thirds of the semester, they have a common deadline for all papers. They read the papers at home, making brief notations to use as a guide in conference. Later in the semester, if and when they feel sufficiently confident, they simply do away with the common deadline and have each paper due at the time of the student's conference. Some teachers follow this procedure for several semesters before switching entirely to inconference reading. A few never do switch; but most experienced conference teachers, at New Hampshire and elsewhere, rely entirely on inconference reading.

There are, of course, limits to what even an experienced conference teacher can accomplish in a given amount of time. The longer the paper, the longer the time needed to read it carefully. At New Hampshire, where weekly papers average five pages in length, the average conference time is fifteen to twenty minutes. Each conference teacher must work out a comfortable balance between the length of the paper and the amount of time needed to read it carefully and confer with the student.

One minor problem about inconference reading is that it is a little awkward, for both teacher and student. The teacher sits there, trying to read the paper, but acutely aware of the student's presence. The student sits there, trying not to stare, but consumed with curiosity. A good way to ease the tension is to give the student something to read—a magazine or another student's paper. The student won't really read it, but it provides a place for restless eyes. To break the silence, the teacher can make an occasional off-hand comment, or grunt encouragingly now and then. These are not matters of enormous consequence, but a conference teacher should not ignore them.

Granted that inconference reading can be effective, wouldn't the ideal situation be a combination of careful at-home reading and individual conferences? I don't think so. Even if it were possible—and it is too time consuming to be practical in most teaching situations—this combination is not so ideal as it might appear. A teacher who has solved all the problems in the paper ahead of time is more than likely to dominate the conference, either through direct statements or leading, manipulative questions. Student comments identify the pitfall here. "He has *really* read my papers and knows what he wants to say." "He seems to almost memorize what he thinks needs improvement." Such extensive prior preparation may awe students but, by effectively excluding them from the critical process, it deprives the conference of much of its special educational value.

The teacher should offer encouragement. This is another truism, one that applies to any type of teaching. Conference teaching is, however, particularly well-suited to encouraging students, and writing is an area where encouragement is particularly necessary.

Many students enter a writing course expecting the teacher to tear their papers to shreds. Their previous experience with writing has been so destructive that they use the word "criticism" with no idea that it could denote something constructive. "He hasn't really criticized my papers. He has just told me what is wrong with them and how I can improve it." "Not much criticism was given. She told me my strong points and my weak points. If I was being criticized, I would not have put much work into my papers." For such students, encouragement from a writing teacher is enormously important. Many students in my study singled out the fact that their teachers had always encouraged them. "She always tries to tactfully point out how the paper can be improved, but she doesn't make me feel like an idiot." "I never feel useless, helpless, or dumb after a conference." The painful sense of inferiority revealed in these comments is, as any experienced writing teacher knows, more the rule than the exception.

Students need the most encouragement early in the semester. The best way for the teacher to provide it is to focus early conferences more on strengths than on weaknesses. There is always something one can honestly praise in a paper; the teacher needs to find it and, if possible, get the student to build on it. Weaknesses should be addressed in the conference only after the student has something positive to develop in the next paper or draft. Since students need encouragement throughout the semester, the basic pattern of strengths before weaknesses is always a constructive way to conduct a conference. It may become predictable, but it is far more effective than its opposite. "Her criticism has sometimes been quite destructive for the simple reason that she points out all the mistakes and bad stuff first, and by the time she gets around to what is good about the paper, the damage is done. Simply reversing the tactic would do a lot more good."

Later in the semester, when the student has gained some confidence and skill, the teacher can begin to focus more heavily on weaknesses, along with the strengths. Some students may become confused by this shift in emphasis, but most can understand and accept it without difficulty. Several students in the study described exactly how the process should work. "As my rewrites became better, her criticism became harsher and down to the finer details." "At the beginning of the course, most criticism was positive, or maybe only slightly negative. Only after she had ensured our trust did her negative criticism become more and more predominant. By then, however, we had realized that she cared about us, and her criticism was worth much more."

This process works best if grading is deferred until at least the middle of the semester. Honest grades early in the semester can be devastating to students, but "encouragement grades" put a teacher in an impossible position later on. A teacher is better off waiting until grades can be both honest and at least moderately encouraging. At New Hampshire, we give a mid-term grade, but base the final grade on a group of papers submitted at the end of the course. We find the mid-term grade a useful device. If some students have mistaken encouragement for evaluation, it shows them what the standards are, while there is still plenty of time to meet them.

The teacher should ask the right questions. The right questions are those that lead the student to become actively involved in the criticism of the paper. The more students participate in the critical process, the faster they become self-reliant, self-sufficient writers. Questioning is the teacher's main device for encouraging and guiding student participation. The right questions can lead a student to respond accurately and honestly. The wrong questions can cause a student to answer evasively, or not at all. The conference teacher must choose questions with considerable care, taking both the individual student and the time of the semester into account.

Early in the semester, many students are still wary of the teacher, uncomfortable in the conference situation and unsure of their writing and critical abilities. To ask such students a question like "What do you think of your paper?" is to put them in a terrible bind. They may like a paper but refuse to admit it because they expect anything they write to be torn to pieces. They may hate a paper but not admit that, either, because they don't want to hurt their grade. The most common early-semester answer to a directly evaluative question is "I don't know." Perhaps some students really don't know, but I suspect most of them are playing it safe, trying not to "look bad" in front of a teacher.

A better way to involve wary, insecure students in the critical process is to ask them questions which do not require direct evaluation. "What's your purpose in this paper?" is the single, most productive question I've found. It is always a useful opener for a conference, with any student, at any point in the semester. Other useful questions are "What parts of the paper do you like the most?" and "What parts of the paper did you have trouble with?" Such questions allow the student to analyze the paper without actually judging it. More directly evaluative questions should eventually be asked, but only when the teacher senses the student is ready to answer them. In the seventh week of the semester, "What do you think of your paper?" is a fair question, and it is more likely to get an honest answer.

Involving students in the criticism of their own writing can be a long and slow process. Students must learn to trust the teacher, the conference method, and their own abilities. They must learn to view the teacher, not as a gradegiver, but as a resource and guide. They must learn to understand that errors and bad drafts are part of everyone's writing process, that their mistakes will not be held against them. They must learn to develop confidence as writers and self-critics. Such profound changes don't happen overnight. Still, if the teacher is patient and asks the right questions, most students can at least begin to make them.

One common tactic for speeding up the process is requiring students to come to conference with written answers to questions about their papers. Students are often able to criticize their papers much better in writing than in the conference itself. This practice can be effective, but it can also produce written equivalents of "I don't know." We can require our students to do certain things, but what we are really after is a fundamental change in their attitude toward their own learning. That change cannot be required; it can only be encouraged, through asking the right questions, then listening patiently for the right kind of answers.

The teacher should evaluate the paper. Several students in the study complained that they never knew how the teacher felt about their papers. "She doesn't take a stand, doesn't tell you whether she loves or hates the paper." "He does not strongly state anything—which is extremely confusing." The major source of this problem was, clearly, the teacher's effort to involve the student in the critical process. A few stubbornly passive students resisted, and resented, all efforts to involve them. "She always asks us what we think are the weak points or areas of our papers—if we knew what they were, we would correct them." This attitude was, however, surprisingly rare. Most students in the study were more than willing to participate in the criticism of their own papers; but they wanted the teacher to be involved in the process, too. "Sometimes I wish she would say a little more about the paper instead of asking me what I think about it." This is a perfectly reasonable complaint. Students have a right to expect the teacher's opinion of their work, and the teacher has a professional obligation to give it.

One student comment raises an important and controversial issue. "Not much help. Carl Rogers type of therapy. 'Well, what do you think?' 'What's your best paragraph?' It's all self-analysis." Charles Duke (1975), using an essentially Rogerian model, has advocated a "nondirective" approach to conference teaching. Duke's article has been influential, and deservedly so; but, while Duke draws many useful parallels between conference teaching and Rogerian techniques, he tends to gloss over the essential difference between a writing teacher and a Rogerian therapist. The teacher's function is to lead students to adopt the teacher's values, the common criteria of good writing shared by the teacher, the English profession, and, with certain wide variations, educated people in general. The therapist's function is to lead clients to clarify or develop their own individual values. Because of this basic difference in function, the writing teacher has the obligation to be more judgmental, and more directive, than a therapist should be in the Rogerian approach.

Despite this difference, the conference teacher can still be, like the Rogerian therapist, a promoter of self-learning. The teacher's task is not to force students to write in a certain way, but to persuade students to adopt certain values by demonstrating their usefulness and validity. To demonstrate how those values can operate, the teacher must be willing to use them in evaluating papers.

The teacher should make specific suggestions for revising the paper. The students in my study expected the teacher's help in revising their papers. Most of them preferred that help in the form of specific suggestions. They valued a teacher's ability to suggest new possibilities and were disturbed when a teacher could not, or would not, do so. "I had some good discussions with her concerning the heart of my paper and what I was trying to convey. She really brought out new possibilities for the paper." "He is willing to discuss revisions, but has trouble finding the possibilities." They didn't want to be told exactly what to do; they expected, and preferred, to choose their own solutions. "No solutions were given, just suggestions. This was good because I felt he expected me to work and learn from that." "She always gives you at least an idea of what to do. She does just enough, without doing it all for you."

Only very few students complained about not receiving explicit directions. This was the clearest example. "Some of the criticism was destructive in that the solution was not told to the student. I must go back and find out what was wrong myself." Quite frankly, it is hard to feel much sympathy for a student who considers it an imposition to be asked to think for one's self. There were more complaints from the opposite point of view, from students who felt the teacher had been too directive. "He also tells us how to change a paper so he will like it. This often changes the meaning of the paper to me." "You may go to her office with a paper on skiing, and she may change everything around so it looks like your paper is talking about snow. If we wanted to write about snow, we would have." This type of complaint I take much more seriously. It indicates that the teacher, not the student, was at fault, that the teacher talked, but didn't really listen. A conference teacher must not only offer suggestions, but listen carefully to how the student is responding to them. A teacher's suggestion becomes a direction, if the student feels pressured to accept it.

The teacher must listen to the student. A conference teacher must know when to talk and when to listen. To offer encouragement and suggestions, to evaluate, to ask questions, a teacher must talk, carefully and tactfully. To encourage student participation, and get the full benefit of it, a teacher must also listen. Of all the skills a conference teacher needs, the ability to listen is easily the most neglected, yet it may well be the most important.

If student participation is desirable, students must be given a chance to participate. If the teacher does most or all of the talking, the student may simply sit there, politely confused. "I often lose my train of thought during some of the instructor's *lengthy* criticisms." The teacher who asks a question must listen to the student's answer. "In conferences, which are so important, she doesn't seem to always concentrate on you. She seems rather to be thinking of her next question instead of listening to the student comment about the writing." Clearly, this teacher was so intent on getting the student to follow her own line of thought that she ignored what the student was actually saying. This is one of the easiest mistakes to make in conference teaching—and also one of the most harmful. It deprives both parties of the benefits of the student's participation, and it violates the very nature of the conference. It changes the conference from a genuine conversation to a form of manipulation.

The students in the study mentioned listening most often in reference to disagreements about a paper. They appreciated the fact that the teacher took their arguments seriously. "If I felt a criticism was unfair, he would explain it further, or listen to me to hear my point of view. He never gave out unfair criticism." While this kind of listening is highly important, there are other, less obvious, ways in which a teacher's ability to listen is crucial to the success of the conference method.

A New Hampshire colleague, Wilburn Sims, has recently made me more aware of one of them. An expert in communications theory, Sims has examined the patterns of student-teacher communication in writing conferences. His findings are quite disturbing. In conference after conference he has found the same basic pattern: the teacher asks a question then ends up providing an answer to it. This process occurs in two ways. In one, the student simply makes noncommittal responses to the question until the teacher finally supplies a direct answer. In the other, the student draws "hints" from the teacher, then "pieces together" an answer that is, in reality, the teacher's own. Sims has noted that teachers seem generally unaware that this process is going on, and often praise their own ideas as original contributions by the student. Sims has not completed his study, and this problem may not be so widespread as his tentative conclusions seem to indicate. Still, it is clear that conference teachers need to listen very carefully to where the ideas in the conference are actually coming from. If they're all coming from the teacher, then the student isn't really participating, just appearing to be.

Perhaps the most common and useful kind of listening a conference teacher can do is what I'd call "listening for clues." Often, a student brings in a draft that is nothing but a mass of raw material, and has no idea of what to do with it. The draft itself may be hopeless, but the material may have potential that the student cannot see. In this situation, the teacher's best course is to discuss the material with the student, listening carefully for signs of special interest on the student's part. If and when the student does show special interest in some feature of the material, the teacher can lead the student to talk about that feature in more detail. Often, as the focus of the discussion narrows, the student can find a topic and purpose for the next paper. This kind of listening is especially important early in the semester, when students see no possibilities in their own material. Possibilities are usually there. The teacher who listens in this way can help students find them.

The six essential tasks of the conference teacher require a variety of skills and virtues: critical ability, common sense, compassion, patience. Not the least of these is simple patience. Conference teaching, as I've defined it, is an indirect method, designed to help students find their own way. Few students find their way quickly. As the conference, or the semester, grows short, a teacher can become sorely tempted to stop questioning and listening and suggesting, and start telling the student exactly what to do. Only the patient can resist this temptation.

A Typical Conference with Good Results

A writing conference is a conversation between a student and a teacher about the student's paper. Since it is, or should be, a genuine conversation, it follows no set pattern; it simply evolves as the two parties talk. Hence, I cannot provide a formula for a successful writing conference, a series of steps to be followed in a certain order. Nor do I want to present a "perfect" conference, one in which the two parties move quickly and neatly to a meeting of minds, lest conference teaching seem much easier than it usually is. A successful writing conference is much more likely to have some false starts and dead-ends in it before a clear agreement is reached. The following conference, taped at the University of New Hampshire last year, is a fairly typical example. It is certainly not a perfect conference—there are at least two apparent dead-ends before the student seems to find a promising direction for his next draft—but it proved to be very helpful to the student. He returned the next week with a much better paper, and made use of all the material generated in the last third of the conference.

This particular conference took fifteen minutes and was held in the teacher's office. It's the eighth week of the semester. A student comes into the teacher's office for his weekly conference. He hands the teacher a four-page paper entitled, "A Life of Music?", then sits down by her desk as she reads it. The paper is a jumble of material with no clear focus or purpose. It is essentially a narrative of the student's experience with music: how he began as a trumpet player in the fourth grade; how he gave up the trumpet and concentrated on singing; how he eventually became a member of the All-Eastern choir in his senior year. Interspersed in the narrative are occasional comments that his schoolmates mocked him and called him "queer" for being interested in singing. The question of the title—should he make a career of music?—receives very little attention: he merely states that he decided not to attend Emerson College, a school which trains people for careers in the various arts, because "music just isn't stable enough" as a profession. The teacher reads the paper through, then begins the conference.

T: O.K., what do you think about this paper?

S: I don't know. I had to write this the night before, but I think it's really bad.

T: This piece is?

S: Well . . . I have so much to say about my music because I've done quite a few things, and so it's really crammed. I could've written a lot more, with more interesting things.

T: I think you've really hit the nail on the head. What you've got here is almost a short chronology of all the things you've done, and I don't think that's the thing you really want us to know about: "Should I go on?"—your music and how you feel about it. I mean, the title is "A Life of Music?" and you don't really address that as much as you could have. I think it's really interesting to see your varied experiences and how professional they really were, but I think you could tighten that section way down.

S: I think with a five-page paper . . . or it would take about a ten-page paper, easily.

T: Yeah, but I'd want you to focus in, though. There's so much in this paper. Why did you decide not to go to Emerson? I think that's something you should tell us more about.

S: They didn't offer me a scholarship or anything. They just offered me an appointment to come in and talk to them, to see what was happening and possibly for some help, because it does cost over $6,000 to go there. A lot of money. I ran into this girl, Jill, last weekend, who's going there, and she's doing a lot of work, and stand-ins in a couple of movies. It's really working out well for her.

T: Did that get you thinking about it again?

S: No, not at all. It's too unstable.

T: Unstable?

S: Yeah, I could end up doing summer stock for the rest of my life, and I don't want to do that. I've done summer stock. I know what it's like—it's not what people think. You get $50 plus room and board, a week, and there's no way you can do anything with your life like that.

T: Unless you just love it so much that you accept that's all you'll ever do.

S: Yeah, and I love musicals a lot, and I love performing in front of people.

T: That's the risk you take, isn't it? And you're not ready to take that risk quite yet? Are you in voice and music here?

S: Oh, yeah! There's some good teachers here.

T: Do you think you could get a good enough professional background here that if you did want to continue, you could do that—or have you given that up?

S: No, I haven't given it up at all.

T: O.K. then, that's what we really want to see here, and that's what's not clear yet: do you want to make music your life, or not? That's the question you're asking, and you very rarely address that in the entire piece. Which leads me to think that either you haven't really, or you have to do a lot more thinking about it to clarify it.

S: I haven't really.

T: I know. I think you have a lot of other things in here you might also want to develop.

S: I'd like to talk more about my All-Eastern experience because that was so fantastic.

T: Your what?

S: The All-Eastern experience—when I went to Washington. That was so great, with so many things happening in a short time, that it's really hard to say anything about it all.

T: O.K., maybe write a paper on just that. I'm sure you could write an entire paper on that if you wanted to. Look at this: "It was a real thrill and I had a real good time." That tells us absolutely nothing. "It was the first time I'd ever ridden on a plane and I was scared to death." Well, that's a little better, but "scared to death" is still a cliche. "The conductor at All-Eastern was a real excellent guy and a fine director." No! [laughter from student] "I made a lot of friends I don't think I'll ever forget." Whoosh! We have nothing to hold on to. Now, what it was—you were trying to compress so much in so little time that you didn't develop anything adequately. So, get all the rest of the junk out. Find the most important things, and then really tell us a lot about those—maybe some of the experiences that changed you, that set you in your commitment to music. Don't give us the strict chronology. Do you think you may have some sense of what you want to do with this now?

S: Yes, possibly.

T: You can tell us what it is to be involved in music—why everyone should be involved in music? Do you want to persuade people?

S: No, maybe just show them.

T: With hope of persuading them to share that?

S: Yes, because they don't know what they're missing. Like you're in the football locker room and a guy's singing—a guy who's supposed to be a "cool" guy—and he's not going to join the chorus; but he has a fantastic natural voice he's never done anything with. Like myself, I've been singing in choirs since fifth grade, but I couldn't sing at all when I started. I had to develop my own voice.

T: I think you've just hit on something else that's really interesting, and something you did spend some time on in the paper, and that is: to a lot of people, singing is "sissy," but it's really not. You might be able to write a piece just on that. And I'm glad you hit on that because I could tell you felt very strongly about that, about moving and being "cool" to be a good football player, and being so "queer" to sing.

S: And all the tough guys who really have good voices.

T: Or who really enjoy singing, on the other hand.

S: It's all rock and roll. But they could sing rock and roll in a choir. We have plenty of pieces that really go, that are that kind of thing.

T: O.K., now here's your original ending: "If it is, maybe some of the so-called tough guys who are against singing and playing instruments, except in a rock and roll band, and who are talented in various fields of music will be singing in choirs. Maybe not. But they will never know what a fantastic feeling of achievement one can feel from making something that has quality." O.K., that's how you ended your piece, but that has nothing to do with your title. So, you see how your piece goes around and around?

S: Yeah, it's really all over the place.

T: O.K., so what do you think you might like to do with it now? I mean, in terms of which thing you want to focus on?

S: I think what I should focus on is the ending. I could leave out the band completely, and go right into the singing, and about how people thought about my singing. I can bring back a lot of things people said—I have a good memory for that.

T: About how singing is sissy and all that?

S: Like, one day I was walking out on the baseball field—I was starting catcher—and the pitcher came up to me and says, "Hey, I hear you made All-Eastern—that's really great." And just the week before, they'd been having this conversation in the corner about how "I don't believe this kid sings."

T: O.K., that's what you want to get into—what it's like to get that constant harassment.

S: That's true. I got it all through school, until the end.

T: Right, until the end, and then, all of a sudden, it's a good thing to do.

O.K., I think this sounds good. I think you've got a better understanding of what you want to do with it now. I think you can focus it a little better. You think about it, and if you get some other ideas, or if you decide to do something different with it, bring it back in and let me know. We'll talk about it some more. Does that sound good?

S: Yes, O.K.

A Conference that Failed

To illustrate more of what I've been saying, I want to present another transcript of an actual conference, a conference that failed to produce an improvement in the paper. I choose this conference as a reminder that conference teaching is not so easy as it might look.

I have two drafts of the paper, one written before the conference, the second written after it. The first draft is a narrative of a week the author, an eighteen-year old freshman, spent with a group of her friends after they had just graduated from high school. This is the opening paragraph.

> Seagulls soaring through the air, waves swaying back and forth, and a cool summer breeze. A typical nice and calm scene from a day at the beach? Possibly, but for me, along with nine other googly-eyed girls who shared a cottage at the beach last summer, nice and calm was far from the case. The events of that week could be better described as nasty and chaotic. Ten girls together for a week means nothing but trouble, but fun trouble it was!

There are ten paragraphs in all. Seven of the middle paragraphs are descriptions of the "fun": how they fooled the realtor to get the cottage, how crowded it was, how hectic their meals were, how much beer they drank, how many boys they met, how wild their parties were. Paragraph seven, which describes the tensions that built up, is the only exception.

> Jealousy was among one of the causes for flare-ups. Those seven days, we also fought about everything from a missing earring to stolen boyfriends. Occasionally, the ramifications were felt through outbursts of anger. One day, after returning from a shopping spree, Robin opened her jacket to reveal to Kim, who had been aggravating her, a T-shirt bearing the message, "You S _ _ _ ." Luckily, similar situations were temporary and the two foes were always friends again within the same hour.

Then it's right back to how "we partied until we were blue in the face (and the head, and the stomach . . .)." This is the conclusion.

> Yet that one week in August was not only one big bash. We all learned about ourselves and each other. Although we spent a great deal of time at each others' throats, the ten of us wild women were never closer in our lives. Oddly enough, that week of sharing closets, clatter, and craziness was one of the best weeks of my life.

Clearly, this is not a very promising draft. It is a pointless narrative by an unusually immature freshman. It has no purpose other than to show how much "fun" the experience was. Perhaps the teacher could have asked the student to show the "fun" in more detail, but detailed accounts of teen-age drinking bouts are just not what college writing is all about. In the conference, the teacher tried to get the student to reflect on the experience, to consider why it was so important to her.

This effort got nowhere. After the conference, the second draft came in almost identical to the first, except for two significant changes. Paragraph seven, the only one devoted to something other than "fun," had been deleted; and there was a new concluding paragraph.

> Yet our fairyland didn't last forever. Eventually the hangovers set in, we started getting on each others' nerves, and it was time to give our cottage over to another unsuspecting party. When I got home, my house never seemed bigger or more welcoming. I truly appreciated everything my home had to offer, from boring nights to strict parents. But if you were to ask me if I would ever share another week's worth of craziness, claustrophobia, and clatter, the answer would undoubtedly be yes, for that was one of

This pious addition of appreciation for "boring nights" and "strict parents" is not particularly convincing, and not in harmony with the rest of the paper.

Perhaps the student was rushed, and the revised draft was a last-minute effort. Perhaps, as seems likely, she was not ready for much heavy reflection. Still, after reading the transcript of the conference, I'm convinced that she could have written an interesting and thoughtful paper about this experience, if the teacher had done a better job.

Here is the transcript of the conference. My commentary is in the notes at the end of this chapter.

T: Do you have any idea where you're going to go from here?

S: It seems like . . . I'm not sure . . . It seems like some of this stuff could be expanded, and I'm not sure exactly what is kind of boring and what I should leave out, because it just involves so much that I . . .

T: The experience, you mean?

S: Right.

T: Okay. Maybe we could make that decision if we talked a little bit about what you mean by "crazy" and "fun." Um, in terms of your experience living at the beach with all these girls, what was crazy about it? Maybe you could list some things on paper.

. . . .

T: I wonder if we could generalize it all—all these things you've listed as crazy.[1]

S: Umm. It was all wild, like, um, chaos or wild. People were coming and going, and you were doing this and when, well . . . I don't know. It was just all these aspects, all these different things—all made it fun; because it was, you know . . . It was so crowded and we partied so much. Little things . . . like having our supper together and everybody was always on the lookout for boys. It just brought us all together and it made it more fun.

T: Humm. Okay, I'm hearing a couple of things. I'm hearing you say that, uh, in all this chaos and craziness, that you developed a kind of group feeling because you were sharing things.[2]

S: Yeah.

T: Okay, well, that's part of it. I want you to write that down. Was it, did it seem real to you?[3]

S: Um? What a funny question! Well, when I look back on it now, it doesn't seem real, but then it was very real.

T: Okay. Maybe I didn't ask the question in a very good way. I was wondering, um . . . it seems like it's really divorced from what your everyday life is like.

S: Oh, yeah!

T: Yeah?

S: It was a complete, like, breakaway. . . . Some of the kids' parents were so strict. And it was just a complete breakaway from home. So, in that aspect, it was like a fairyland. They had no parents, no anything.

T: Okay. Now that might be something you'd want to touch on. Um, "fairyland" is sort of an interesting word—sort of a never-never land. Is it a place you'd like to stay forever? (Pause) Why not?

S: Because it takes such effort.

T: Physically?

S: And mentally. Your body can only take so much and after a while . . . but it was a good release, like that . . .

T: "Release" is an interesting word, too. I think people do need kinds of releases like that, or visits to fairyland, or whatever you want to call it. Um, maybe that's what you mean by "crazy"—that it was just so removed from anything familiar. Your meals weren't at the regular time and your food wasn't gotten or procured in the same way, you didn't sleep in a regular place or at regular times, you weren't living with your family, you were living with all these girls. . . . So that might be what you mean by "crazy." Okay?

S: Okay.

T: Now that also might be what you meant by "fun." And I think you mentioned a group feeling. Well, that might be something you'd want to emphasize in the paper.[4]

S: But, along with that group feeling, there were always personality conflicts and, uh, other conflicts.

T: Okay.

S: Another thing I was thinking about is how different characters develop. There was one girl who was always on, like . . . We had a cottage alcoholic and a cottage flirt and, um, there were different characters like that evolved.[5] But I . . .

T: Didn't know how that fit?

S: Yeah.

T: Well, I guess that's kind of what we're talking about now—what you want to make the main point of the paper. So you can make some decisions on what fits and what doesn't fit. Okay?

S: Maybe I ought to just forget about that. That was just an idea.

T: Well, no, I don't think you ought to forget about it because . . . what I see us doing now is looking at some more complicated aspects of what that week was. You know, what it did to people and what it represented to people. And, um, before, you were pretty much talking about the physical parts of it—how it was crowded, and how you partied, and how you looked for boys . . . um, but you didn't really talk about what that meant to people or what that seemed like to people.

S: Oh, yeah.

T: Do you see what I mean?

S: Yep.

T: Okay, and I see you beginning to explore that idea now.

S: Oh, yeah.[6]

T: What about you? What did it mean to you?

S: Um, well it, to me, it was just an experience.[7] You know, being with my friends and being in such close contact with them and it just . . . I don't know . . . I learned a lot about myself.

T: What did you learn?

S: As far as what I can and can't . . .

T: Take?

S: Yeah.

T: Okay.

S: And also, like, living that close to somebody, you're gonna learn . . . I mean—ten girls! It was kind of *the* clique from high school. And you kind of learned really who your friends are and, you know, which ones aren't your friends.[8]

T: All right. That might be an interesting central point to the paper. What other things did you learn?[9]

S: Uh . . .

T: You said you learned what you could take and what you couldn't take.

S: Yeah.

T: And you learned what your limitations were or what lines you were willing to draw for yourself.

S: Exactly. Like, how far I would go.

T: Did it surprise you?

S: Kind of. Well, it didn't really surprise me. It just sort of brought myself out. Like, I knew. Well, I thought I could go that far, but I wasn't sure.

T: What are you talking about—going that far?

S: Like as far as, well . . . maybe doing a favor for somebody, or maybe doing crazy things at four o'clock in the morning.[10]

T: Maybe it did surprise you.

S: Well, I did do some crazy things, now that I think about it.

T: And liked them?

S: Yeah.

T: So, that might be something you'd like to explore in the paper: what you learned about yourself. Do you have that written down? I keep pushing you to write things down just in case you're like me.

S: No. I, ah, really like it—it helps.

T: Okay. So, you have two things there: who your friends are, and something about your own limits in, maybe, lots of ways—how crazy and uninhibited you were going to be.[11]

S: So, are you saying this is more physical stuff and I should get into, kind of like, psychologically, aspects of it? Like emotions? Things like that?

T: Yeah, I guess that's kind of what I'm saying. I think the physical part is interesting; but I think it's more interesting to be able to apply what's in here. I guess, if I were working on the paper, I would take one of these big ideas here—these two—and then look through the paper, and then see which examples help you expand that idea, and, then, which ones don't. Okay?

S: Yeah.

T: And you might want to try both of these.

S: Yeah.

T: I think it's going to be a totally different paper now.

S: Yeah.

T: You're using this as base material to get into another thing. I don't think I would like to use this about friends.[12] Okay, how about this one?

S: I like this idea—you know, how far I'd go. I just went wild, uninhibited.

T: You said some of the girls came from very strict families?[13]

S: Yeah, like there was this one girl who always had to be in by eleven, and she just went crazy.

T: Like how?

S: There was no word to describe it. So, in that case, it was a total social release for her.

T: You might think in terms of your own social release—was there any for you?[14]

S: Um . . .

T: And what were they? And what did you learn about yourself from that?

S: Okay.

T: It seems to me it's going to be a little heavier paper now.

S: Yeah, heavy!

T: But, I think, more interesting.

S: All right. Should I keep this stuff in?

T: You have to measure all the stuff in this paper against whichever idea you decide to work on. Let's see if we can take an example. Okay: "I learned how far I would go." (Pause) You may have to restructure some of your examples to fit. Let's say, drinking. Did you learn anything about how you felt about drinking? Did you like it or not? Was it worth it? That's the way I would look at the examples.

S: Okay. I kind of like this idea about how it's a release, though.[15]

T: Yeah. Okay. I think that is interesting. Um, I have a lot of dogs and my dogs were never on a leash until . . . Well, I never had trouble getting my dogs to follow me. They always stayed pretty close; but friends of mine who had dogs who'd never been off the leash had trouble with the dogs running away and not coming back again. In fact, we took a dog like that and, within three months, the dog didn't wander off. And now I can put a leash on or I can not put a leash on. But, I think there is a comparison that can be made here: that, if restraints are loosened, why, people go wild. I'm not sure if that's terribly relevant. But, to what extent did this happen to you, if at all?

S: No, I think that's relevant.[16] I think that would be a good point, then. Do you think that would work?

T: Yeah, I think it could work. I think that it could be a really interesting paper that way.

S: Okay.
T: And you could also tie in the part of what you learned from it.
S: Oh.
T: What you learned about your own self-restraint or developing it, or the need for it, or . . . I don't know. Whatever you want to do with it! But you could tie those two things together, the learning part and the release part.
S: Okay. Good enough.
T: Thank you for coming in.
S: Thank you.

Some of the problems in this conference seem unique to the particular situation. The teacher's personal questions put both parties in awkward positions at times. First, the student seems to avoid specific details; later, the teacher seems to.

The basic problem, though, is all too common. The teacher began with an open, supportive stance and ended up being highly directive. She did so because she didn't really listen to the student. She heard the student's idea about group relations—at least, she acknowledged it four times—but she was not alert to the possibilities in it. The student brought it up repeatedly, and was eager to supply specific details. These were strong "clues" that the subject had potential. The teacher didn't hear them. Nor did she seem to hear how unresponsive the student was to the idea about self-limits throughout most of the conference. The teacher kept on pushing that idea until she ended up virtually forcing it on the student. The revised draft is the worst of both worlds. The student has dutifully removed her own best paragraph, and almost all other traces of the idea she seemed most interested in. She has used the teacher's idea only in a pious conclusion which belies the spirit of the whole paper.

With the benefit of hindsight, I like to think I would have done better. Don't we all?! We would have picked up those clues, drawn out the material that was so obviously there, and gotten that student to write a fine paper. It all seems so easy, in retrospect. But conference teaching is not easy. We all make the same mistakes this teacher made. We miss opportunities. We talk, and don't listen. It's so hard to be patient in conference sometimes, so frustrating to sit there listening to students struggling to find an answer we already see. How easy it would be to give them the answer, the neat solution to the problem. We'd be happier. The students would be happier. They just wouldn't learn as much.

Notes

1. The omitted segment consists of nineteen brief exchanges. In it, the student, in response to questions, lists the "crazy" things and writes them down. The written list is as follows: "chaos, crowdedness, partied so much, getting cottage, having supper, searching for boys." Since all of these things were already in the paper, this forced recapitulation seems pointless to me. Presumably, the teacher's point was to lead the student to "generalize."

2. This is an accurate restatement of an idea the student has just expressed, an idea about group relations. That idea is not, however, the general definition of "craziness" the teacher has been seeking.

3. Rather than develop the student's idea about group relations, the teacher continues to press for a definition of "craziness." Her question clearly throws the student off track.

4. The teacher has now arrived at definitions of "crazy" and "fun," but only by providing them herself. The student's "Okay" is a minimal response. Perhaps sensing that the student isn't with her, the teacher returns to the student's own idea about group feeling.

5. Paydirt! The student has suddenly come to life. She has volunteered some general ideas and begun to give some specific examples. This is what a conference teacher should always be listening for.

6. Three straight minimal responses from the student. Why has she backed off? Probably because the teacher has jumped in to generalize and intellectualize about what the experience "meant to people." Perhaps, if the teacher had held back and drawn out more specifics about "personality conflicts" and "different characters," the student might have been encouraged to develop some general ideas of her own. The teacher has tried to be helpful, but she has "come on too strong" and smothered the student's initiative.

7. Once again, the teacher has taken the initiative and the student is perplexed.

8. The student takes the initiative back and returns to her idea about group relations.

9. The teacher acknowledges the student's idea, but brushes it off and continues on the track *she* is interested in.

10. The teacher has put both of them in an embarassing position. If the student has really "gone too far" in any significant way, she's not going to tell the teacher about it. Nor would the teacher be eager to hear it. The teacher's question was irresponsible. The student may well have "nothing to hide" anyway, but her answer is safely bland and vague. Perhaps relieved, the teacher does not press for further details, and moves quickly back to generalities.

11. The teacher summarizes the two main ideas that have come out of the discussion: "who your friends are," the idea the student volunteered, and "something about your own limits," the idea the teacher has been pushing.

12. Here, the teacher rejects the student's ideas "about friends," and, in effect, directs the student to use the teacher-proposed idea about "limits."

13. The student finally shows some enthusiasm for the teacher's idea, and seems ready to provide some personal examples after all. For some reason, though, perhaps because she doesn't really want to hear them, the teacher quickly shifts the focus to the other girls.

14. The student has dutifully supplied a promising specific about another girl and, lo and behold, the teacher shifts back once again to the student's own case. After this last shift, the student lapses back into a noncommital "Okay." I don't blame her. I can't, for the life of me, figure out what the teacher is doing here, and I don't see how the student could have, either.

15. The student still shows some interest in the idea of "release," a word she herself introduced into the discussion. Rather than drawing out the student, the teacher breaks in with the long analogy.

16. The student claims to find the analogy "relevant." I can't help wondering how much this analogy contributed to the safe and conventional ending of the revised draft. The underlying moral of the analogy is that, given enough freedom, an individual will stay safely home. That's exactly the moral of the revised ending. Is the student, in her revision, simply telling the teacher what she wants to hear?

8 Writing in the Total Curriculum: A Program for Cross-Disciplinary Cooperation

Robert H. Weiss
West Chester State College

Virtually all departments of English in colleges and secondary schools now prepare students for academic writing in advanced courses. This mission is both formidable and delicate. As teachers of writing, we work in a context of service to other departments and are accountable in ways that teachers of physics and history are not. Our composition students enter academic disciplines and postgraduate occupations. It is impossible for us to be well informed about the kinds of writing demanded in even a small number of these. The good writing that we see our students produce is not in itself a sufficient accomplishment. Sometimes we are held responsible for subsequent work that we rarely or never see, and over which we have no direct influence. For these (and other good) reasons we often argue that composition instruction is a responsibility to be shared by all teachers in all departments.

The arguments for sharing are sensible, not fabricated to get English teachers off the hook. Since composing skills tend to atrophy if they are not used, the work of even the most excellent of writing teachers may not "take" without complementary exercise in other disciplines. Writing done as part of the struggle for learning achievement has a readily comprehensible purpose. If writing essays—short impromptu ones in examinations or long research ones in term papers—does indeed help students to learn by enabling them to synthesize information or to scrutinize it from several perspectives, then faculty in the content areas have a vested interest in teaching students to write in such traditional academic genres. If preparation for content-related writing is the chief end of the composition course—an assumption with which few of our colleagues would disagree—then instruction in the specialized writing forms familiar to them should follow or supersede instruction in the "literary" forms familiar to us: narration, description, exposition, and persuasion. The implicit appeal of these arguments for teachers in other departments is not that their participation in writing instruction will necessarily improve their students' writing, but that it will improve their students' learning.

Our mission actually challenges us to revise a curriculum in which we are central; to create not just a course but a complete program, and not a program confined within the department of English but one extending outward and involving faculty members in other departments. The program may consist of consultations among faculty, informal workshops, or formal seminars; of voluntary "faculty development" activities or curricular requirements; of team-teaching, course pairings, or course clusters; of special training for writing teachers to serve particular areas of a discipline, or of reciprocal training for content teachers to give writing courses in their departments. It may be connected with some kind of writing center offering support services to students, faculty or both. Such a global program can have many names: writing throughout or across the curriculum, as the British phrase it; interdisciplinary writing; or cross-disciplinary writing. I prefer the latter phrasing because it is brief and does not imply lofty interdisciplinary studies or degree programs bridging several academic disciplines.

This chapter explores some ways in which teachers can cooperate in cross-disciplinary efforts to improve student writing, first in composition courses, then in the content area.

An English Course for a Cross-Disciplinary Writing Program

Because composition courses have no fixed content and no standard body of materials to be studied, they are often cross-disciplinary in a sense. The traditional anthology of essays from diverse disciplines represents the willingness of English teachers to satisfy their obligation to the general curriculum; but it does not reflect any shared responsibility for student writing. This is true also of the thematic course covering an area of intellectual interest (love, the environment, fringe religions); of the career-oriented course (Writing for Engineers); and even of the composition course which is paired with a content course to provide students with subject matter for their writing. While these course types have the advantages of interesting students in subject matter and of preparing them better for subsequent studies, the English department as ever remains solely responsible for writing instruction.

A general writing course, serving a broad range of academic disciplines or postgraduate professions but not attached to any of them in particular, would overcome the limitations of current offerings. Some courses with such a purpose now exist, and more are planned. But before the new effort is installed firmly in the curriculum and perpetuated in textbooks, we need intelligent debate, based in solid theory and research.

The ideal cross-disciplinary writing course, as I see it, originates with an English instructor who surveys and consults with the entire faculty to discover what kinds of writing they actually assign. Related research would survey a wide variety of courses. (Such research is now being considered by several of my estimable colleagues.) A writing course could then be devised which would simulate the writing conditions and constraints found throughout the entire curriculum. Course readings would include only samples of the writings gathered in the survey and would set the stage and establish models for assignments. In this way the readings would preface what the students were asked to write more directly and closely than in traditional composition courses. Writing assignments would be related to the types of writing the students will likely encounter in other disciplines, rather than being based on a theoretical classification of the kinds of writing. The general cross-disciplinary writing course would be a rhetorical sampler. There might be a process analysis essay in history, an examination question in biology, a memorandum in engineering, an abstract in psychology, a proposal in social welfare, and so on. Traditional theme-writing would be assigned only if the survey found it frequently in academic courses or anywhere else—in other words, not at all.

The prototypical text for a cross-disciplinary writing course would be a book touching all of the academic disciplines—both liberal and applied. Yet an author trying to organize a text according to the numerous categories of academic and practical writing would produce chaos. Under one cover, no text could adequately deal with laboratory notebooks and reports, literary analyses, surveys of secondary sources, book and article reviews, proposals, critiques, research reports, case histories, constitutions, feasibility studies, nursing "processes," logs, journals, field notes, lesson plans, policy statements, observation reports, summaries, abstracts, and memoranda (hardly an exhaustive list). Since many of these genres mix informative, persuasive, and expressive purposes in varying proportions, and since the range of audiences also varies, the four traditional rhetorical modes would make no sense as an organizing principle either. The sheer varieties of writing in school and at work would seem to call for an encyclopedia rather than a single text, an entire writing curriculum rather than a course.

A more plausible approach is this: given the purpose, occasion, tone, and audience of a piece of academic or practical writing, English instructors could concentrate on the choices of language, logic, and structure the writer must make. Although not the only legitimate problems for a writing course, these are usually construed as the major ones by schools and employers. Moreover, if students are to focus on all of the options before them in a writing situation, they should be given a full and authentic context for writing and full and authentic information to write about, not just brief guidelines for carrying out a task. This means that to provide students with writing practice as well as advice, we should elevate the writing assignment to a place of primacy in the writing text and course. Our texts should be thin and contain few maxims, as E. D. Hirsch argues in *The Philosophy of Composition* (1977). They should include a good selection of contextual assignments that embody those few precepts we would teach—not be like the comprehensive but unteachable "rhetorics" and "handbooks" before us today.

One way for an English course to fulfill these goals is to present students with a number of authentic case situations that call for them to write in a full range of forms, for a variety of academic and nonacademic audiences and purposes, with a variety of tones, and from a variety of perspectives (voices or personae). The cases should illustrate the materials and structures and tones available to novice and practiced writers in those forms. In a highly focused case situation detailing real people, events, and motives, students are given a role that includes writing to a specific audience and (usually) for a utilitarian purpose. A true-to-life dramatic fiction is established, providing context, constraints, and options for the writer, as well as a functional problem-solving objective for each assignment. Some cases can be completely self-contained units—banks of data to be processed in writing—while others can be vehicles for invented solutions or for research. Each case integrates rhetorical precepts and issues of composition pedagogy into the contextual information and the language of the assignments, but without identifying them as such.

Cases have the power of authenticity and are not as artificial as other academic exercises. In composition as in content courses, cases can provoke active inquiry and discussion by their very nature as open-ended writing problems faced by real people. A case assumes an answer to the question "Why write?" It can be a bridge connecting any academic area to writing. Traditionally, a case approach is used in such fields as medicine, law, science, psychology, and business, so a request from an English teacher to help develop cases that call for writing should be well received in a number of departments. Of course, composition students would only be getting a foretaste of such fields. Rather than simply studying the case content, they would attend to the forms, principles, and strategies required to compose it in the case situation. A case which calls for translating a medical article into plain English can yield valuable lessons on audience analysis, technical and plain language, and paraphrase; a case which considers the constitutionality of legislative initiative and referendum can help instruct students to analyze a process; a case which establishes perception and introspective analysis as prerequisites for a job candidacy can illustrate observation and the use of detail; and a case set in the business world can be a vehicle for teaching thesis-and-support structure.

A writing course based on cases, or on any other approach steeped in subject matter related to the academic curriculum, would represent a notable form of service for an English department. It would also be a graceful means to achieve collaboration among departments, one that could well encourage further cooperative endeavors. Indeed, if the problem of teaching writing is larger than can be solved through any course of study in English, and if writing instruction is best when it exists within a larger framework which gives it direction and nurture, a composition course like the one I have just described could have important "political" benefits. By demonstrating one department's willingness to bend in the direction of others, it would be a powerfully persuasive example of the desirability of a writing program reaching across the curriculum.

English as Advisor to Other Disciplines

For a cross-disciplinary writing program to be successful, writing must hold an important place in an institution's routine, writing experiences must be numerous and varied in kind and purpose, and good writing must be defined wisely and rewarded consistently. Good thinking—perhaps the sole purpose of education—must be equated at least roughly with good writing; conversely, good writing must be seen as good thinking, not mere conformity to codes of grammatical, lexical, and orthographic etiquette. This does not mean that English teachers abandon either their humanistic heritage or their jobs, nor that other teachers become grammarians or learn the discipline of composition. Rather, it means that English departments may realize the hope so often expressed that our efforts will be supported and reinforced (and perhaps rewarded) by our colleagues.

Such a comprehensive program means a climate in which good writing will thrive as a matter of course, and not be a luxury. This is not an enterprise to be simply legislated into existence. It must be developed out of concern for the purposes and functions of writing and for the relation of writing to grammar, usage, and mechanics—and to speech. It should also reflect coherent theories of how writing skills develop. Undertaken with these goals in mind, this program would actually enlarge the responsibilities of the English faculty, who have or can readily gain the knowledge to implement it. They would no longer serve the rest of a school or college in a restricted fashion, as with a writing center or a remedial program to which poor writers are remanded. Rather, they would be actively engaged in supporting the faculty at large in the use of writing assignments that fulfill their diverse instructional goals.

To give the best advice, we should know our audience, why they want our advice, and what they expect to hear from us. Most faculty members appear to be "writing conservatives," people who think of writing solely as a means of communication. Responding in predictable ways to various pressures on them, including the general media commentaries on literacy and their echoes in the professional as well as academic journals, these teachers are encouraged to assume the posture of the rigorous schoolmaster of bygone days and to try to enforce high standards of articulate, correct expression. They tend to show little tolerance for error; to some it is a distasteful confirmation of the cultural inferiority of the times. Many simply do not know how, or can not recollect what it is like, to write perfect academic prose under pressure. Their attitudes show little respect for the writing process. At best, faculty "conservatives" can help to produce good writing by creating an environment in which it is expected. At worst, they might pose a problem by returning freshman English to the weeding-out function of twenty years ago. Without guidance and advice, therefore, they are not really prepared to participate in writing instruction.

There is also a smaller faculty contingent of "writing progressives" whose awareness of the intellectual and emotional growth that can come with writing makes them more tolerant of the inevitable error and inelegance in student work. They accept the idea that writing is itself a route to new knowledge, not simply a device to express or communicate what is already or should be known. These teachers are often ready to do things that characterize the "liberated" kinds of composition teachers: to use writing in class; to assign prewriting exercises and rough drafts; to hold conferences with their students; to teach the essay exam; to require their students to keep academic journals; and to consider voice, audience, and situation in writing assignments. They are often eager to evaluate formatively, that is, to guide students to improvement through revision, rather than merely to test and grade their performance. As with the "conservatives," some of these teachers are themselves good writers, some poor ones.

Our advice must be fitted to the whole spectrum of faculty in order to influence it toward common goals—without polarizing it, as has occurred in many English departments, over the goals themselves or the methods of attaining them. We must speak both abstractly and practically, never introducing "methods" or "materials" as gimmicks but only as they fit our best theories, supporting research, and experience. Issues in our profession (for example, students' rights to their own language) should be clarified by openly discussing opposing views with our colleagues in the content areas. This guidance can only increase their sensitivity to the effects their teaching and evaluation can have on student writing and speaking. Yet not all such issues, nor all features of composition instruction, are adaptable to all content courses (picture the psychology instructor with ninety students who tries to focus on rhetorical modes, holds writing conferences, or asks students to consult a compendious handbook on usage). We must select wisely the advice we feel most serviceable proximately and important remotely.

On the level of theory, we should ask content instructors to consider what the purposes of writing assignments should be—communicative or expressive, learning or testing—and whether student responses should be judged for their quality of writing as well as for their content. Theoretical questions of purpose quickly become issues of practice: how many papers to assign, what sort, how to evaluate them. Should their purpose always be communicative—to test the students' knowledge? Should the audience always be the teacher? Should long papers be assigned to determine the student's prowess at amassing and organizing a large body of information? Or should a series of shorter, analytical papers be assigned to obviate plagiarism? Can "expression" or "form" be separated from content, and how much should it count toward a student's grade? Must all student writing be evaluated? Can some of it be evaluated by other students? Should performance on a given date be evaluated, or might periodic cumulative evaluations guide students to higher levels of performance? The answers to some of these questions will become broadly applied policies: others will appeal only to individual teachers. Given a field so rich in ideas and practices as composition, English teachers have much to offer their colleagues in other departments. They can provide a variety of suggestions both traditional and innovative, both standard and experimental.

Advice in the Traditional Mode

The essay examination is the typical embodiment of the timeworn purpose of school writing: testing. Teachers in content area incorrectly assume that their students know how to take essay tests and are often disappointed with the essays they receive. These teachers can be shown how to improve the instructions they give students, how to explain very clearly what they expect, and how to provide rhetorically equivalent tasks when choices are available. They will be happily surprised to learn that process analysis may be a simpler mode than definition. They can also take a cue from composition instructors who use models of student or professional writing. Well before an examination, they can use the overhead projector and/or dittoed handouts to illustrate what they consider excellent. They can also identify what they admire in such a performance: its clear presentation of a dominant idea, its analysis of the idea's components, its marshalling of detailed evidence, its logical relation of the data to the key idea, its movement toward an affirmed conclusion, its clarity of expression. They can have their students make rank order evaluations of essay responses, and even develop a set of essay scales. Confronted with student-produced samples of work ranging from A to F, and given the opportunity to discuss them, students can formulate and sharpen their ideas of competent writing. This kind of teaching does not take too much class time if it produces significant student achievement; it may even be an effective way to introduce and teach a new topic.

Similarly traditional but effective advice can significantly improve teachers' understanding of the term paper—and of why and how students should do this standard school assignment. There are teachers who will frankly admit never having thought about this. They believe students should write term papers, but have not scrutinized their belief. There are some who simply distribute a list of general topics for long papers and expect their students to carry the ball thereafter. These practices can be redressed if teachers come to recognize that they should justify the lengthy assignments they make, and that they can only test the ability to compose at length about a technical subject within a discipline is they prepare students for the exercise and give them proportionately full guidance, something more than a sheet of instructions accompanied by a few minutes of talk.

This approach presents the task as a learning experience. A number of practical suggestions from the standard repertory of English instructors can deepen the learning experience: students can be taken to the library, shown how to use the card catalogue, indexes, abstracts, government documents, and other materials pertinent to research in the field. It is also helpful if they hear comment on the overall organization of long papers in the discipline, and on how to introduce and conclude them. Outlining is worth suggesting as well as other organizing techniques. The system of attribution to be used—parenthetical textual references or footnotes—should be explained and illustrated. Since research and experience demonstrate that student writing improves when instructors comment on it, commentary on one or more drafts before a finished product has every chance of yielding a superior final version. As one of my colleagues somewhere across the curriculum put it, "Before, being a perfectionist, I had to ask sixty to seventy percent of my students to rewrite their term papers; now, however, my commenting on their rough drafts has reduced that rate to under ten percent. A little guidance from me really pays off."

By demonstrating to colleagues that we can cooperate on *their* terms, we can then proceed to illuminate more significant issues of language, grammar, and writing. In other words, rather than let the movement "back to basics" put us in the position of commending unworkable and unfortunate practices whose efficacy has been disproved time and again, we should take advantage of our role as consultant and guide, seize the opportunity to enlighten and persuade, and strive to develop the kind of total writing envionment that will improve student attitudes to writing and writing performance. If asked to provide other departments with style manuals or correction sheets, we should consent to do so; but when we write them, we should not simply rehash the overgrown handbooks that lay out everything so carefully, condescendingly, and boringly, and so often in defiance of several decades' worth of information about language. We should instead turn our colleagues' attention to issues of assignment-making, language variety, error as distinct from inelegancy, supportive ("formulative") commentary on student papers, and the practices our research has demonstrated to be effective for short and long term improvement of student writing.

Innovative Ideas

Several of our profession's most innovative practices are likely to be accepted readily by some content instructors. Three of these in particular are profitable: teacher modelling, peer involvement in various stages of the writing process, and conferencing. Each may be used in teaching the customary academic genres or more practical rhetorical forms.

If a teacher spends class time writing out an essay exam answer or an article's conclusion, the class benefits immensely by seeing how it is done—and by seeing the false starts, the choices to be made, the way a writer progresses toward a not-quite-clear goal. If the best teachers of writing are those who themselves write, and if one of the most dramatic and forceful ways to illustrate the writing process for students is to write before their very eyes, to compose on the blackboard, then content instructors who wish to give some writing instruction can do so simply by becoming models. As advocated and successfully practiced through the Bay Area Writing Project, teachers who themselves write tend thereby to be sympathetic to student problems, including the personal struggles of a writer confronted with an assigned rather than self-generated task. They will also be aware of the shortcomings inherent in the writing task ("I couldn't say what I wanted to," "The topic bored me," "Other things were more important"). Students who can watch teachers of biology, philosophy, or social work compose will possess vivid models of true writing triumphs and failures.

In addition to learning to write from observing and imitating their instructors, students in content courses can also learn from assisting one another in structured ways in prewriting and post-writing. Peer critiquing has the disadvantage of taking up class time but the benefit of improving student practice without excessive teacher effort—always a key consideration. If we can persuade content instructors that assigning much writing tends to improve writing quality, that only obsessed teacher-martyrs believe that they have to read or evaluate all assigned writing, and that any feedback on a writing assignment tends to help the writer improve, then they are free to assign 10,000 words or more per semester, and, without feeling guilty, to evaluate only a small portion of them. Peer evaluation can occur in a content course in small groups which exchange papers, with all students reading short papers aloud to the others and receiving feedback, or with all students carrying one anothers' papers home for review.

A content instructor can also break a class into small groups of students for peer review/criticism, for writing on different perspectives of a course issue, and for assuming roles in a course-related situation. Some of the discussion sessions can be taped so that students have a verbal record as the basis for developing or revising a written assignment. As with peer tutoring in composition classes, the more adept writers can be given responsibility for assisting the others who feel they need help. A checklist reflecting the particular concerns of the content instructor may be used by the class as a whole or by peer evaluators.

Conferencing can also be done by content instructors. If they can be inspired to hold at least one conference with each student in the process of writing, as well as to make themselves available for subsequent trouble-shooting or band-aid conferences, they will almost surely be more satisfied with the quality of work submitted to them. A system of rough drafts followed by conferences would be ideal, but at least some person to person exchange over the students' writing can abate many of the writing-related problems of content faculties.

Evaluation and Placement

Composition teachers can also aid an academic department in using writing to evaluate students for entry into the major or into advanced courses, or for writing proficiency as an exit criterion. For small numbers of students and teachers, a checklist of writing skills developed according to clearly defined rubrics is probably sufficient, provided that the writing features itemized and the number of determinations of quality for each item are kept short. While English teachers may be comfortable in analyzing all of the characteristics of a piece of writing (for example, paragraph development, sentence structure, word choice, and punctuation) and in making subtle discriminations for each feature (with tags like *mature, acceptable but indistinctive, incoherent, childish*), we can hardly expect colleagues in other disciplines to share our expertness in critical reading of manuscript. However, we can suggest a brief list of writing features for acceptability.

Aside from a category for the evaluation of ideas, such advice might produce a checklist like the following:

	Yes	*No*
Do the generalizations make sense?	____	____
Are they adequately supported by evidence?	____	____
Are the paragraphs linked to a dominant idea?	____	____
Do the sentences "flow"?	____	____
Are word choices appropriate?	____	____
Are grammar, spelling, and mechanics appropriate?	____	____

With such a form, an academic department should then be able to test incoming students and identify students who would benefit from individual attention, remedial work, or an honors program. This evaluation is best conducted not by individual professors but by a team, which would reflect a departmental consensus and minimize the idiosyncracies of individual raters. The same system could be used for exit proficiency examinations.

For large numbers of students, holistic evaluation of writing is most feasible. A large department can be prepared by one or more composition instructors to a point of considerable accuracy in doing quick, first-impression evaluative readings of impromptu assignments. After initial preparation, ten instructors can dispatch with 500 brief essays in about three hours, whereas analytic reading and scoring (two readings of ten minutes each) would take about two full work days. Initial preparation time would be only a few hours, and the time for subsequent standard-setting exercises with the same readers would be shorter.

Writing to Learn

The most compelling argument to other faculty for upgrading the writing environment is that it may lead to improved learning achievement. A writing regimen is really a learning regimen, whether in just one course of study or in an entire school program. Not all faculty members are troubled by the quality of writing they see, yet all can be presumed to be concerned about increasing the learning power of students. Some will accept the argument that writing produces learning, but they invariably do so as an act of faith or on the evidence of personal experience. The relationship of writing to learning has not been demonstrated in ways that satisfy doubting administrators and faculty members reluctant to prescribe or participate in a "writing curriculum."

English teachers and other humanists assume (as I did when I first started teaching literature twenty years ago) that writing reinforces, fixes, or even produces learning. Yet that assumption, which logically places writing and the writing teacher at the center of the curriculum, is based strangely enough in those most unimaginative and unstimulating of school exercises: essay examinations, book reports, term papers, short papers, and the like. Rationales for what some psychologists call the mathemagenic—learning inducing—effects of writing typically refer only to these and similar genres of academic writing, certainly never to the kind of thing produced in a journalism course or poetry workshop. Phrased another way, the assumption is that doing formal transactional writing, a highly complex communicative activity drawing on cognitive reservoirs, increases cognitive retention or produces new cognition. This may have been so for those of us who as students were highly literate. That it may also be so for others I doubt. The assumption does justify the habitual (and comfortably unexamined) practice of schools and colleges. But we have Moffet, Britton, and Emig to tell us that writing is developmental, self-expressive and self-concerned before it can be outward-looking and self-effacing, and we have Piaget, Bruner, and other psychologists to tell us that all learning proceeds personally ("affectively"). Both sets of theories persuade that the traditional school writing assignment is indeed not the best writing mode to induce learning. We know that such tasks as essay examinations and term papers are met by students, even high-achieving students, as threatening ordeals, on which depend grades, status, careers, prestige, life. Whatever the real value of these tasks, we should put the lie to their justification as learning experiences.

Writing exercises accompanied by less apprehension are probably far more fruitful as learning inducements or reinforcers and may be assigned in addition to or instead of essay tests and long research papers. If the more that students become involved in a subject, the more they can learn it, then encouraging or requiring frequent or continuous writing related to that subject is a potentially excellent teaching device. This is especially true if some of that writing is expressive or speculative, the kind which Britton (1975) claims is "best adapted to exploration and discovery" because it "externalizes our first stages in tackling a problem or coming to grips with an experience." Only writing that is engaged, not threatening, involves the imagination and links with learning.

Writing engagedly about a subject may be the ultimate "study skill." If a writing regimen can work to produce learning, the writing done need not be error-free. Acquisition of content is independent of linguistic punctilio, even of rhetorical appropriateness. Writing done in a cross-disciplinary writing program might take place *between* evaluations of the learning. If content instructors give many brief writing tasks about their subject in a variety of modes, encourage personal expression, and abandon puritanical concern to read or attack what is said therein or how, they may well be improving their students' retention and discovery of concepts, attitudes to writing and learning, and writing performance itself.

One effective exercise is writing clarity statements. It consists of immediate and brief written responses to a lecture, discussion, or reading, and may take either of two forms: (1) a personal statement that a concept is clear or confusing to the student, and why, or (2) a brief answer to a question presented by the teacher to interrupt or end a class, or as a homework assignment. Clarity statements may be done more conveniently on 3 x 5 cards and turned in to the instructor than entered in an academic journal or notebook. Then the teacher has an immediate opportunity to respond, to monitor what students are learning, to establish dialogue about points coming across well or cloudily. Teachers who use clarity statements find that students are not satisfied with merely filling the cards. Rather, they write all over the place, ask direct questions of the teacher, and desire additional space. This is engaged writing and engaged learning. Observing it is delightful; participating in it is exciting.

And it is a far different cry from that of the English (or other) professor who piously expostulates to colleagues that assigning papers is a better test of learning (synthesizing, analyzing) than a short-answer quiz. It is also far removed from the practice of most English teachers in their literature or language courses. We, as well as our colleagues, will have to experience this use of writing before we will convince ourselves of its practicality. Yet the idea is not really new, as can be seen in Rollo Walter Brown's 1915 study, *How the French Boy Learns to Write.* The key is to immerse students in writing: to have them daily respond in writing to questions posed by the teacher, to have them review and rework their notebooks, to have them keep an academic journal separate from or as a part of their notebooks, to nurture all sorts of writing in addition to formal modes, to direct them in reading and assisting one another's writing.

The Writing Environment

Understanding how writing assignments can be real vehicles for learning is vital for teachers of composition even though we have historically devoted our attention to other concerns—how writing develops thinking, how it expresses feeling, how it communicates. Yet it is we who may be called upon to assist content teachers in developing students who can write intelligently (and correctly) about an academic subject; we should be prepared to meet that request. Composition was entrusted to English departments almost by accident. Few English teachers were taught to be teachers of writing, and many English teachers prefer not to teach composition courses. Nevertheless, the theories, research, and collective experience of our discipline, especially in recent years, make us the only logical source of these writing-related ideas and practices. Model methods for excellent instruction in writing are gradually emerging from what is known and promulgated, and significant features of these may be modified for instructors in any academic disipline.

The features most promising for successful transfer of knowledge about writing to the academic disciplines can be summarized as follows. Writing done for school can have various purposes, forms, and audiences. All of it need not be done for the traditional purposes of testing or disciplining students, nor need it consist exclusively of the traditional forms (book reports, research papers, essay examinations). Some of it may be expressive—personal, speculative, even "creative" or poetic. (The chair of my college's Department of Earth Sciences recently confided to me his desire—not just willingness—to have the students in his introductory course compose poems and short stories.) Some school writing can specify audiences other than the teacher and can be action-oriented rather than informative. Much of this writing need not be evaluated; some which is written to "count" can be evaluated in rough draft stages. Instructions for most assignments should be made painfully clear. Commentary on student papers should not be vague, condescending, or predominantly negative. Finally, all teachers can teach something about the appropriate language, rhetorical patterns and purposes, research tools, and mechanical conventions for writing in their disciplines.

None of these suggestions requires special training in grammar, rhetoric, or composition, nor that the teacher be an excellent writer or critic of writing. The sole prerequisite is that a teacher experiment with writing assignments and writing instruction as part of the quest for improved learning. Teachers who abandon the habit of requiring only impersonal, transactional writing can help to create an environment in which writing is a student's friend, an aid to learning. This calls for them to give writing assignments regularly, to be aware that writing is a process, to evaluate writing constructively, to vary the purpose or mode of assignments so that personal expression is permitted or encouraged, to illustrate or model the kinds of writing wanted or not wanted, to preface a writing task with instructions and with the kind of strategy discussion or activity that characterizes "pre-writing," and to teach the organization, logic, word choice, and mechanical considerations of the "language" of their discipline.

Creating a writing environment will produce long-term improvement in the quality of student writing, although not necessarily in ways incrementally noticeable in any one classroom. Demanding good writing and proscribing errors yields satisfactory results with a few students—those most like ourselves. But since the key to writing improvement is a combination of positive attitude and positive achievement, a comprehensive program for nurturing writing will be more satisfactory in producing genuine improvement in greater numbers of students. Achievement in learning can be increased through writing, and positive attitudes to writing can be encouraged by the adoption of our best techniques of composition instruction in content courses.

We do indeed have allies in our desire to improve student writing. We must offer them a program grounded in theory, research, and collected experience. To exert the most beneficial influence on the total curriculum, to become better advisers for both the communicative and heuristic uses of writing, we may have to probe our own purposes and methods as writing teachers, educate ourselves about writing as it is done outside of English classes and writing centers, and reform our own courses and textbooks. We must enable others to see writing humanistically, as a bridge to meaningful expression and learning in all school work.

References

Introduction

Bizzell, Patricia. "Thomas Kuhn, Scientism, and English Studies." *College English*, 40 (1979), 764–771.

Britton, James, et al. *The Development of Writing Abilities 11–18.* London: Macmillan Education, 1975.

Coles, William E., Jr. "Teaching the Teaching of Composition: Evolving a Style." *College Composition and Communication*, 28 (1977), 268–270.

Cooper, Charles, and Lee Odell. *Research on Composing: Points of Departure.* Urbana, Ill.: NCTE, 1978.

Emig, Janet. *The Composing Process of Twelfth Graders.* Urbana, Ill.: NCTE, 1971.

Fogarty, Daniel. *Roots For A New Rhetoric.* New York: Teacher's College Columbia University, 1959.

Graves, Donald H. *Balance the Basics: Let Them Write.* New York: Ford Foundation Papers on Research About Learning, February, 1978.

Graves, Richard L., ed. *Rhetoric and Composition, A Sourcebook for Teachers.* Rochelle Park, N. J.: Hayden, 1976.

Kuhn, Thomas S. *The Structure of Scientific Revolutions.* 2nd ed. Chicago: University of Chicago Press, 1970.

Langer, Susanne K. *Philosophy in a New Key.* 3rd ed. Cambridge: Harvard University Press, 1957.

Murray, Donald M. *A Writer Teaches Writing.* Boston: Houghton Mifflin, 1968.

Neel, Jasper P., ed. *Options for the Teaching of English: Freshman Composition.* New York: Modern Language Association, 1978.

Tate, Gary, ed. *Teaching Composition: 10 Bibliographic Essays.* Fort Worth, Tex.: Texas Christian University Press, 1976.

Tate, Gary, and Edward P. J. Corbett, eds. *Teaching Freshman English.* New York: Oxford University Press, 1967.

Tate, Gary, *Teaching High School Composition.* New York: Oxford University Press, 1970.

Young, Richard. "Paradigms and Problems: Needed Research in Rhetorical Invention." In *Research on Composing: Points of Departure.* Ed. Charles R. Cooper and Lee Odell. Urbana, Ill.: NCTE, 1978

Chapter One

Chomsky, Carol. "Write First, Read Later." *Childhood Education,* 47 (1971), 296-299.

Emig, Janet. "The Biology of Writing: Another View of the Process." In *The Writing Processes of Students.* Ed. Walter T. Perry and Patrick J. Finn. Report of the Annual Conference on Language Arts, State University at Buffalo, Conference Report #1, 1975.

Graves, Donald H. "An Examination of the Writing Process of Seven-Year-Old Children." *Research in the Teaching of English,* 9 (1975), 236-45.

King, Martha L. "Research in Composition: A Need for Theory." *Research in the Teaching of English,* 12 (1978), 193-202.

Perl, Sondra. "Unskilled Writers as Composers." *New York University Education Quarterly,* 10 (1979), 17-25.

Sommers, Nancy I. "The Need for Theory in Composition Research." *College Composition and Communication,* 31 (1979), 46-49.

Stafford, William. "The Minuet: Sidling Around Student Poems." *Field,* 18 (1978), 49-56.

Chapter Two

Berke, Jacqueline. *Twenty Questions for the Writer.* 2nd ed. New York: Harcourt Brace Jovanovich, 1976.

D'Angelo, Frank. "Imitation and Style." *College Composition and Communication,* 24 (1973), 283-290.

Davis, Vivian I. "Toward a Model of the Composing Process." *Arizona English Bulletin,* 19 (1976), 13-16.

Emig, Janet. "On Teaching Composition: Some Hypotheses as Definitions." *Research in the Teaching of English,* 1 (1976), 127-35.

Flower, Linda S., and John R. Hayes. "Problem Solving Strategy and the Writing Process." *College English,* 39 (1977), 449-461.

Gallo, Donald R., ed. "Teaching Writing: Advice from the Professionals." *Connecticut English Journal,* 8 (1977), 1-31.

Garrison, Roger H. "One to One: Tutorial Instruction in Freshman Composition." In *New Directions for Community Colleges.* San Francisco: Jossey-Bass, 2 (1974), pp. 55-83.

Gorrell, Robert M. "Question II, 7." In *Questions English Teachers Ask.* Ed. R. Baird Shuman. Rochelle Park, N. J.: Hayden, 1977, pp. 58-60.

Hall, Donald. *Writing Well.* 3rd ed. Boston: Little, Brown and Co., 1979.

Larson, Richard L. "Teaching Rhetoric in the High School." *English Journal,* 55 (1966), 1058-1065.

Larson, Richard L. "Structure and Form in Non-Fiction Prose." In *Teaching Composition: 10 Bibliographical Essays.* Ed. Gary Tate. Fort Worth, Tex.: Texas Christian University Press, 1976, pp. 45-71.

Moffett, James. "Learning to Write by Writing." In *Teaching High School Composition.* Ed. Gary Tate and Edward P. J. Corbett. New York: Oxford University Press, 1970, pp. 43-60.

Murray, Donald M. *A Writer Teaches Writing.* Boston: Houghton Mifflin, 1968.

Neel, Jasper P., ed. *Options for the Teaching of English: Freshman Composition.* New York: Modern Language Association, 1978.

Ong, Walter J., S. J. "Literacy and Orality in Our Times." In *Profession 79.* New York: Modern Language Association, 1979, pp. 1-7.

Payne, Lucile Vaughn. "Teaching Students to Write." *National Education Association Journal,* 55 (1966), 28-30.

Shaughnessy, Mina P. *Errors and Expectations.* New York: Oxford University Press, 1977.

Squire, James R., and Roger K. Applebee. *High School English Instruction Today.* New York: Appleton-Century-Crofts, 1968.

Zinsser, William. *On Writing Well: An Informal Guide to Writing Nonfiction.* 2nd rev. ed. New York: Harper and Row, 1980.

Chapter Three

Britton, James N. *The Development of Writing Abilities (11-18).* London: Macmillan Education, 1975.

Chomsky, Noam. *Language and Mind.* New York: Harcourt Brace Jovanovich, 1972.

Creber, J. W. Patrick. *Sense and Sensitivity.* London: University of London, 1965.

Elbow, Peter. *Writing Without Teachers.* New York: Oxford University Press, 1973.

Judy, Stephen, Geoffrey Summerfield, Richard Peck, and Patrick Courts. *The Creative Word I-IV.* New York: Random House, 1973, 1974.

Judy, Stephen. "Writing for the Here and Now." In *Explorations in the Teaching of Secondary English.* New York: Dodd, Mead; Harper and Row, 1974.

Jung, Carl. *Man and His Symbols.* New York: Dell, 1968.

Langer, Susanne K. *Philosophy in a New Key.* 3rd ed. Cambridge: Harvard University Press, 1957.

Macrorie, Ken. *Uptaught.* Rochelle Park, N. J.: Hayden, 1970.

McLuhan, Marshall. *Understanding Media.* New York: McGraw-Hill, 1973.

Miller, James E., Jr., and Stephen Judy. *Writing in Reality.* New York: Harper and Row, 1978.

Moffett, James. *Teaching the Universe of Discourse.* Boston: Houghton Mifflin, 1968.

Murray, Donald M. *A Writer Teaches Writing.* Boston: Houghton Mifflin, 1968.

Piaget, Jean. *The Language and Thought of the Child.* New York: New American Library, 1955.

Vygotsky, Lev Semenovich. *Thought and Language.* Trans. Eugenia Hanfmann and Gertrude Vakar. Cambridge: The MIT Press, 1962.

Chapter Four

Cooper, Charles R., and Lee Odell. *Research on Composing.* Urbana, Ill.: NCTE, 1978.

Corbett, Edward P. J. *Classical Rhetoric for the Modern Student.* 2nd ed. New York: Oxford University Press, 1971.

Emig, Janet. *The Composing Process of Twelfth Graders.* Urbana, Ill.: NCTE, 1971.

Emig, Janet. "Writing as a Mode of Learning." *College Composition and Communication,* 28 (1977), 122–28.

Festinger, Leon. *Theory of Cognitive Dissonance.* Stanford, Calif.: Stanford University Press, 1965.

Guilford, J. P. "Creativity: Yesterday, Today, and Tomorrow." *Journal of Creative Behavior,* 1 (1967), 3–8.

Kinneavy, James L. *A Theory of Discourse.* Englewood Cliffs, N. J.: Prentice Hall, 1971.

Kinneavy, James L., John Cope, and John Campbell. *Aims and Audiences in Writing.* Dubuque, Iowa: Kendall/Hunt, 1975.

Kinneavy, James L. *Writing—Basic Modes of Organization.* Dubuque, Iowa: Kendall/Hunt, 1976.

Koestler, Arthur. *The Act of Creation.* New York: Macmillan, 1964.

Lauer, Janice M. "Heuristics and Composition." *College Composition and Communication,* 21 (1970), 396–404.

Lauer, Janice M. "Invention in Contemporary Rhetoric: Heuristic Procedures." Diss. University of Michigan, 1967.

Lauer, Janice M., Gene Montague, Andrea Lunsford, and Janet Emig. *The Worlds of Writing.* New York: Harper and Row, 1980.

Lonergan, Bernard. *Insight: A Study of Human Understanding.* New York: Philosophical Library, 1957.

Nystrand, Martin, ed. *Language as a Way of Knowing.* Toronto: Ontario Institute for Studies in Education, 1979.

Ong, Walter J., S. J. "The Writer's Audience is Always a Fiction." *PMLA,* 90 (1975), 9–21.

Piaget, Jean. *To Understand is to Invent: The Future of Education.* Trans. George-Anne Roberts. New York: Grossman Publishers, 1973.

Polyani, Michael. *Personal Knowledge: Towards a Post-Critical Philosophy.* New York: Harper and Row, 1958.

Rohman D., Gordon and Albert Wiecke. *Prewriting: The Construction and Application of Models for Concept Formation in Writing.* Cooperative Research Project #2174, Cooperative Research Project of the Office of Education, U. S. Department of Health, Education and Welfare, 1964.

Rothenberg, Albert. "Creative Contradiction." *Psychology Today,* June, 1979, pp. 55–62.

Searle, John R. *Speech Acts: An Essay in the Philosophy of Language.* London: Cambridge University Press, 1969.

Tate, Gary, ed. *Teaching Composition: 10 Bibliographic Essays.* Fort Worth, Texas: Texas Christian University Press, 1976.

Vygotsky, Lev Semenovich. *Thought and Language.* Trans. Eugenia Hanfmann and Gertrude Vakar. Cambridge, Mass.: The MIT Press, 1962.

Wallas, Graham. *The Art of Thought.* New York: Harcourt Brace Jovanovich, 1926.

Winterowd, W. Ross. *Contemporary Rhetoric: A Conceptual Background with Readings.* New York: Harcourt Brace Jovanovich, 1970.

Young, Richard E., Alton Becker, and Kenneth Pike. *Rhetoric: Discovery and Change.* New York: Harcourt Brace Jovanovich, 1970.

Chapter Five

Abrams, M. H. *The Mirror and the Lamp.* New York: Oxford University Press, 1953.

Baird, Theodore. "The Freshman English Course." *Amherst Alumni News,* 40 (1952), 194-96.

Bruner, Jerome. "On Perceptual Readiness." *Psychological Review,* 64 (1957), 123-152.

Bruner, Jerome. *On Knowing: Essays for the Left Hand.* 1962; rpt. New York: Atheneum, 1965.

Bruner, Jerome. *The Process of Education.* 2nd ed. Cambridge, Mass.: Harvard University Press, 1977.

Burke, Kenneth. "Rhetoric—Old and New." *Journal of General Education,* 5 (1951), 202-209.

Burke, Kenneth. *Permanence and Change: An Anatomy of Purpose.* 2nd revised ed. Indianapolis: Bobbs-Merrill, 1965.

Coles, William E., Jr. "Freshman Composition: The Circle of Unbelief." *College English,* 31 (1969), 134-42.

Coles, William E., Jr. *Teaching Composing.* Rochelle Park, N. J.: Hayden, 1974.

Coles, William E., Jr. *The Plural I: The Teaching of Writing.* New York: Holt, Rinehart and Winston, 1978.

Dewey, John. *Experience and Education.* 1938; rpt. New York: Collier Books, 1963.

Dowst, Kenneth. "What the Composition Teacher Composes: The Writing Assignment as Teaching Device and Work of Art." *Arizona English Bulletin,* 20, No. 2 (1978), 99-103.

Dowst, Kenneth. "Epideictic and Englishpaperese: A New View of an Old Style." *Freshman English News,* 7 No. 3 (1979), 21-24.

Gibson, Walker, ed. *The Limits of Language.* New York: Hill and Wang, 1962.

Gibson, Walker. *Seeing and Writing: Fifteen Exercises in Composing Experience.* 2nd ed. New York: David McKay, 1974.

Langer, Susanne K. *Philosophy in a New Key.* 3rd ed. Cambridge, Mass.: Harvard University Press, 1957.

Lanham, Richard A. *Style: An Anti-Textbook.* New Haven: Yale University Press, 1974.

Kinneavy, James L. *A Theory of Discourse.* Englewood Cliffs, N. J.: Prentice Hall, 1971.

Miller, James E. *Word, Self, Reality: The Rhetoric of Imagination.* New York: Dodd, Mead & Company, 1973.

Ohmann, Richard. "In Lieu of a New Rhetoric." *College English,* 26 (1964), 17–22.

Richards, I. A. *The Philosophy of Rhetoric.* Galaxy ed. New York: Oxford University Press, 1965.

Sapir, Edward. "Language." In his *Culture, Language, Personality: Selected Essays.* Ed. David G. Mandelbaum. Berkeley: University of California Press, 1956, pp. 1–44.

Whitehead, Alfred North. "The Organization of Thought." In *The Aims of Education and Other Essays.* New York: Free Press, 1957, pp. 103–119.

Chapter Six

Elbow, Peter. *Writing Without Teachers.* New York: Oxford University Press, 1973.

Shaughnessy, Mina P. "Basic Writing." In *Teaching Composition: 10 Bibliographical Essays.* Ed. Gary Tate. Fort Worth, Tex.: Texas Christian University Press, 1976, pp. 137–167.

Shaughnessy, Mina P. *Errors and Expectations.* New York: Oxford University Press, 1977.

Wiener, Harvey S. "An Open Not a Revolving Door." *The London Times Higher Education Supplement,* July 13, 1973, p. 14.

Wiener, Harvey S. *The Writing Room: A Resource Book for Teachers of English.* New York: Oxford University Press, forthcoming.

Wolfe, Don Marion. *Creative Ways to Teach English.* New York: Odyssey, 1966.

Wolfe, Don Marion. "A Realistic Writing Program for Culturally Diverse Youth." In *Education of the Disadvantaged.* Ed. A. Harry Passow. New York: Holt, 1967, pp. 415–423.

Chapter Seven

Benjamin, Alfred. *The Helping Interview.* 2nd ed. Boston: Houghton Mifflin, 1974.

Clark, William A. "How to Completely Individualize a Writing Program." *English Journal,* 64 (1975), 66–69.

Cooper, Charles R., "Teaching Writing By Conferencing." In *Survival Through Language: The Basics and Beyond.* Proc. of the Twenty-ninth Language Communication Conference, 1976. Ed. Rita Bean, Allen Berger, and Anthony Petrosky. Pittsburgh, Penn.: University of Pittsburgh, 1977, pp. 7–22.

Duke, Charles. "The Student-Centered Conference and the Writing Process." *English Journal,* 64 (1975), 44–47.

Fisher, Lester, and Donald M. Murray. "Perhaps the Professor Should Cut Class." *College English,* 35 (1973), 169–173.

Garrison, Roger H. "One to One: Tutorial Instruction in Freshman Composition." In *New Directions for Community Colleges.* San Francisco: Jossey-Bass, 2 (1974), pp. 55-83.

Jacobs, Suzanne E., and Adela B. Karliner. "Helping Writers to Think: The Effect of Speech Rate in Individual Conferences on the Quality of Thought in Student Writing." *College English,* 38 (1977), 489-505.

Murray, Donald M. *A Writer Teaches Writing.* Boston: Houghton Mifflin, 1968.

Petrosky, Anthony R., and James R. Brozick. "A Model for Teaching Writing Based Upon Current Knowledge of the Composing Process." *English Journal,* 68 (1979), 96-101.

Rogers, Carl R. *On Becoming A Person.* Boston: Houghton Mifflin, 1961.

Chapter Eight

Beyer, Barry K. "Pre-writing and Rewriting to Learn." *Social Education,* 43 (1979), 187-89, 197.

Beyer, Barry K. and Anita Brostoff. "The Time It Takes: Managing/Evaluating Writing and Social Studies." *Social Education,* 43 (1979), 194-197.

Britton, James, et al. *The Development of Writing Abilities 11-18.* London: Macmillan, 1975.

Brown, Rollo Walter. *How the French Boy Learns to Write.* 1915; rpt. Cambridge, Mass.: Harvard University Press, 1965.

Emig, Janet. "Writing as a Mode of Learning." *College Composition and Communication,* 28 (1977), 122-27.

Field, John P., and Robert H. Weiss. "Cases for Context and Involvement: Giving Students Part of the Action." *Bulletin of the Pennsylvania Council of Teachers of English,* 38 (1978), 3-8.

Frase, L. T. "Boundary Conditions for Mathemagenic Behaviors." *Review of Educational Research,* 40 (1970), 337-348.

Hancock, Deborah Osen, and Andrew Moss, eds. *Reading and Writing Programs within the Discipline: A Preliminary Directory of Models.* rev. ed. Fullerton, California: University of California and California State Universities and Colleges Joint Work Group, 1979.

Hirsch, E. Donald. *The Philosophy of Composition.* Chicago: University of Chicago Press, 1977.

Klinger, George. "A Campus View of College Writing." *College Composition and Communication,* 28 (1977), 343-47.

Martin, Nancy, et al. *Writing and Learning Across the Curriculum 11-16.* London: Ward Lock Educational, 1976.

Miles, Josephine. "What We Compose." *College Composition and Communication,* 14 (1963), 146-154.

Moffett, James. *Teaching the Universe of Discourse.* Boston: Houghton Mifflin, 1968.

Rothkopf, Ernst Z. "The Concept of Mathemagenic Activity." *Review of Educational Research,* 40 (1970), 325-335.

Van Nostrand, A. D. "Writing and Generation of Knowledge." *Social Education*, 43 (1979), 178–80.

Weiss, Robert H. "The Humanity of Writing." *Improving College and University Teaching*, 27 (1979), 144–147.

Weiss, Robert H. and Michael Peich. "Faculty Attitude Change in a Cross-Disciplinary Writing Workshop." *College Composition and Communication*, 31 (1980), 33–41.

Writing Across the Curriculum Project Pamphlets. National Association for Teachers of English. London: Ward Lock Educational, 1973–76.

Zemelman, Steven. "How College Teachers Encourage Students' Writing." *Research in the Teaching of English*, 11 (1977), 227–34.

Contributors

Thomas A. Carnicelli is Professor of English at the University of New Hampshire and has been director of Freshman English since 1973. A noted medieval scholar, he has also authored articles on the uses of literature in Freshman English and has given numerous workshops and papers describing the individual-conference method. He is co-director of the UNH-Westbrook College Summer Institute for Two-Year College Writing Teachers.

Timothy R. Donovan is Associate Professor of English and chair of Freshman English at Northeastern University, Boston. He is also a Research Associate at the NEH Institute on Writing at the University of Iowa, and is co-director of the Martha's Vineyard Summer Workshop on Teaching Composition. He has authored a number of articles on composition pedagogy, writing program administration, and teacher training in composition.

Kenneth Dowst is Assistant Professor of English at the University of Iowa, where he is a staff member of The Institute on Writing and a teacher of courses in writing, the teaching of writing, and literature. He formerly taught at the University of Pittsburgh, where he worked with William E. Coles, Jr., in developing the epistemic approach. His publications include two textbooks for correspondence courses in writing and a number of articles on writing theory and pedagogy.

Paul A. Eschholz, Professor of English at the University of Vermont, has authored dozens of articles and reviews. He has edited or coauthored ten titles, including *Language Awareness* (St. Martin's Press, 1978), *Subject and Strategy* (St. Martin's Press, 1978), and *St. Martin's College Handbook of English* (St. Martin's Press, forthcoming). He edits *Exercise Exchange: A Journal for English Teachers in High School and College.* For the past two years he has directed The Vermont Writing Program, an NEH Project.

Stephen Judy is Professor of English at Michigan State University. He has taught in public schools, at the University of British Columbia, and Northwestern University. He was editor of *The English Journal* 1973-1980. He is author of *Explorations in the Teaching of English* (Harper & Row, 1975), *Writing in Reality* (with James E. Miller, Jr., Harper & Row, 1978), *The First Two 'Rs: Reading and Writing in America* (Oxford, 1979), *The English Teachers' Handbook* (Winthrop, 1979), *English Today and Tomorrow* (Hayden, 1979), and *The ABCs of Literacy: A Guide for Parents and Educators* (Oxford, 1980).

Janice M. Lauer is Professor of English at Marygrove College and director of the Writing Program at the University of Detroit. In addition to authoring articles for scholarly journals, she has contributed to *Contemporary Rhetoric: A Conceptual Background With Readings* (ed. by Ross Winterowd, Harcourt Brace Jovanovich, 1975) and *The Four Worlds of Writing* (coauthored central chapters with Gene Montague, Harper & Row, forthcoming). For the last three years she has directed the Rhetoric Seminar at the University of Detroit.

Ben W. McClelland is Associate Professor of English and department chair at Rhode Island College, Providence. He developed Rhode Island College's composition program, including its Writing Center, program of placement testing, and curriculum. He has consulted on composition program development, has served as an NEASC accreditation team member, and has written on composition teaching and on academic administration.

Donald M. Murray is both a writer and a teacher of writing. He has published novels, nonfiction books for both adults and juveniles, articles, short stories and poetry, won the Pulitzer Prize for editorials written for the *Boston Herald*, and served as an editor of *Time*. A Professor of English at the University of New Hampshire, he developed a basic, university-wide composition course and teaches, besides writing courses, a seminar in the teaching of writing. He has published numerous articles on teaching writing in professional journals. Editor/author of *Write to Communicate: The Language Arts in Process*, he is also author of a textbook for teachers of writing, *A Writer Teaches Writing* (Houghton Mifflin, 1968).

Robert H. Weiss is Professor of English at West Chester State College and is project director for "Strengthening Writing in the Humanities and Across the Curriculum" (NEH grant). He has initiated a number of state and national programs and panels on interdisciplinary writing. He is the coauthor of *Cases for Composition* (Little Brown, 1979) an interdisciplinary approach to writing.

Harvey S. Wiener is Professor of English at LaGuardia Community College (CUNY) and has developed various writing curricula at LaGuardia, Penn State, and Springfield Gardens High School, Queens. He is the author or coauthor of *The Short Prose Reader* (McGraw Hill, 1979), *Any Child Can Write* (McGraw Hill, 1978), *English Skills Handbook* (Houghton Mifflin, 1978), *Creating Compositions* (McGraw Hill, 1977), and many other texts and articles in writing and literature. He is currently president of the National Council of Writing Program Administrators.